IN PRAISE OF
MADNESS

Realness Therapy—
The Self Reclaimed

IN PRAISE OF
MADNESS

Realness Therapy—
The Self Reclaimed

by Paul J. Stern

<small>WITH THE ASSISTANCE OF</small>

Charles C. McArthur

W · W · NORTON & COMPANY · INC ·
New York

Library of Congress Cataloging in Publication Data
Stern, Paul J
    In praise of madness.
    1. Mental illness. I. Title.
RC460.S76   616.8'9   72-3181
ISBN 0-393-01056-2

CONTENTS

PREFACE

Everyone has a right to a self of his own. It would seem that this right is inalienable, but in actual fact it is elusive, easily lost sight of. Only a fortunate few among us can truthfully claim to be the owners of our own soul. The paradoxical fact is that this self, which is at the core of our being, is not given to us ready-made. It needs to be discovered. And appropriated. During the slow, laborious process of growing up, much conspires against our actualizing this most precious of our gifts.

To take full possession of his self, a human being must have received in childhood the bounty of lavish parental love which validated him by taking delight in his mere existence. Most children are made to earn part of the love which is their natural due. Earned love is counterfeit love.

But the child has no choice. He will take any facsimile of love, if the genuine article is not available, and he will pay for it with his soul. Heroically, and pathetically, he will try to make himself into what his parents want him to be. In exchange, he will be given tokens of approval masquerading as love. This is the ferocious bargain, the deadly contract, on which much of family life is built.

The contract is not explicit, nor need it be. In the world of emotion, the child is the true linguist. He understands without having to be told. It is the parents who, as a rule, are blind to what is going on. *They* believe in the myth of their essential benevolence, and it is true that, usually, they are not motivated by malice or low Machiavellianism. It simply happens that to the extent that they are neurotically impoverished, they *must* remake the child, reduce him to being a tranquilizer, go-between, appendage, toy, vicarious liver, entertainer, performer, and, most perniciously—a parent. The parents' neurotic anxiousness impels the child to become predictable and, in the process, to become a stranger to himself.

A college girl who described her childhood home as a "magnolia-scented concentration camp" understood the nature of the tacit family contract: "Sure, they loved me. I just had to be rearranged a bit." As part of the process of rearrangement, the girl's mother persuaded her, when she was twelve, to have her nose bobbed. She had experienced this surgical beautification of her face as the ultimate indignity, the most tangible mark of the embezzlement of her self.

Most of us do not have to go to the extreme of esthetic surgery to present a more pleasing image to our parents. But in order to survive, most of us have had to forswear, or put in hock, some parts of our selves. These disowned, splintered-off fragments of the self constitute the haunting unrealities which seize and overwhelm the psychotic person during the acute psychotic break, which obtrude themselves in the guise of symptoms upon the neurotic, and which hover, more discreetly, at the periphery of the lives of those who pass for healthy.

This haunting but often elusive unreality is, at bottom, nothing but a reality, or potentiality, which was denied. At the time it first occurred, this denial was often an act of self-preservation. But for the person to become himself or —which is the same—to seize his own reality, he must exorcise his ghosts by embracing them. He must appropriate the reality of his unreality. Contrary to the cozy notions of common sense, Reality is not given to us once and for all; it does not exclusively belong to anybody, nor is it the communal property of everyone.

The present book looks at some of the forms in which the unreal that demands to be real presents itself, notably the hallucinatory reality of those we call mad, and the dream reality of the sane and insane alike. It examines some of the pseudo-realities—such as the opium of violence and the self-violation of drug use—by which those who are psychically straitjacketed attempt to impale themselves upon a reality which eludes their grasp. And, finally, its last chapter describes psychotherapy as a process by which men may overcome their unrealness. By resolutely vindicating our unreality, instead of continuing to deny it, and by gently inviting it to have its say, we may still recover what was once our inalienable birthright: a self of our own.

9

IN PRAISE OF
MADNESS

Realness Therapy—
The Self Reclaimed

1

MADNESS

The Realness of the Unreal

When the everyday world of a person suffers a sudden, catastrophic collapse, and when from its ruins he is assailed by voices which cannot be localized or by visions which have no tangible origin, we say that the person is mad (or psychotic). We tend to think of his altered way of being as illness, and of the uncanny phenomena he encounters while in this state as hallucinatory or *unreal*. What do we mean when we say that a voice heard by a person is unreal?

The statement that a person "hallucinates" the presence of a voice does not, as a rule, mean to deny the "subjective" part of the experience of hearing. The person does in fact hear something. If we question him on this, he will emphasize the immediacy and distinctness of his auditory perception. What we refer to, then, is the lack of an "objective" counterpart, the absence of a voice out there in the common world which could be heard by others. What we mean by unrealness is that the hallucinatory voice is private and exclusive. Like the nightly movie performances we call dreams it can be directly experienced by one person, and one person alone. Its reality is a reality of one.

Now surely this way of defining realness, by correspondence with something "objective" in the "outside world," is not the only possible one. There is a lot to be said for the alternate notion, underlying much popular psychology, which holds that real is *whatever affects me*, even if I cannot identify or make tangible its source. The German language expresses this idea most directly in that *Wirklichkeit* (reality) and *wirken* (to have an effect on) share the same word stem.

There is no law of logic which compels us to assume that events taking place in a private space, accessible only to one person, are by this very fact unreal. There is certainly nothing in the immediate experience of the "hallucinating" person which bears out such an assumption. On the contrary: if there is one feature that is characteristic of psychotic perception it is its immediate (self-evident) convincingness. The psychotic reality grabs the person by the throat, as it were; it overwhelms him in a way which leaves no room for doubt about its realness. Such doubts arise only afterward, when the person re-emerges from his altered world, and, looking back, reflects upon his experience.

This belated doubt about the realness of what befell him serves, first of all, a psychological function. It is meant to put distance between the person and his uncanny experience. Reality, in its psychotic mode, has committed a veritable rape against him. To play down the seriousness of the injury, he stigmatizes the events that caused it as "unreal." In doing so, he does not give a mere description; he makes a judgment. He denies, and at the same time obliquely admits, his horror at having been overwhelmed. And his doctors, his family, and other emissaries from the "sane" world are usually, for reasons of their own, only too ready to support his denial. In fact, should he prove unreasonable, unwilling to recant his psychotic revelation, they will probably try, more or less subtly, to elicit a retraction.

Thus we see that to label something actually experienced as unreal is, in a sense, an attempt at exorcism. It is a way of telling an unwelcome visitor to be off. And to most men those experiences are peculiarly unwelcome which put into question the very foundations—such as the notion of an "objective" reality—upon which their everyday world is built.

But the person who tries to deny the reality of highly charged experiences by calling them deluded or hallucinatory may have to pay a high price for this evasion. By consigning the alien experience to the twilight zone of fictitious happenings, he will disavow, and force underground, a crucial part of himself. The uncanny, disembodied voice and the intangible visionary experience ought to be heeded not only for their positive content but for the challenge which their mere presence poses to the prepsychotic reality of the person. If this (seemingly normal) reality had not been seriously defective, the "hallucinatory" phenomena could not have taken over in their peculiarly flagrant, harrowing way. Hence the most general message of the psychotic experience, prior to all particular contents, is: "You who are seared by me must change your life!" The return to the state before the breakdown, so diligently sought by patients and would-be helpers alike, is precisely the one thing which ought to be excluded.

This, at any rate, will be our position throughout this book. Going even further, we shall maintain that the ghosts of unreality, wherever and in whichever shape they arise, ought not to be anxiously held at bay and, by our de-realizing them, denied admittance. On the contrary, we shall argue that they ought to be received with open arms, as it were, and given their fullest scope. Only by meeting the uncannily alien with this open, hospitable stance shall we be able to overcome the hauntedness which is typical of our relationship with denied, unrealized possibilities of being; only in this way can we surpass, rather than suppress, our own unrealness.

The unreality of madness as a possible way station on the road to an enriched reality: this notion has been enthusiastically embraced by parts of the counterculture, has been oversold and falsely romanticized by it. Not every psychotic break leads to a breakthrough. Far from it. A series of psychotic eruptions may reduce psychic life to the stony deadness of a burned-out crater. The catastrophe of calcification and deadening of the personality is always a possible aftermath of deep regression. Even in more benign cases, the struggle for the renewal of the old reality, by the appropriation of the unreal, is difficult, the outcome hazardous.

Let us illustrate some basic aspects of this struggle by two contemporary case histories with fairly happy endings. (Or so we may judge, even though in this instance it is particularly true that only the completion of the life history by death enables us to make a judgment of this kind with any degree of finality.) The first case is in the public domain; it involves the poet Allen Ginsberg, himself a midwife, spokesman, and idealized guru of the counterculture. Ginsberg, in copious writings and interviews, has grappled eloquently with the issues of psychotic dread and psychotic daring. The second case is that of an anonymous young woman who described with great poignancy her endeavors to come to terms with some visionary experiences.

In 1948 Allen Ginsberg, then in his early twenties, had an ecstatic experience which became a turning point in his life. Ginsberg has described many times the crucial event, labeled by some a hallucinatory psychotic episode. He has emphasized that it was "natural," as opposed to drug-induced. (Apparently at that time drugs had not yet come into his life in a big way.)

Ginsberg was lying on his bed one summer afternoon, his eyes idling over Blake's poem "Ah Sun-flower," which he had read innumerable times, to the point of dullness, when all of a sudden something odd happened: the over-familiar, outworn verse sprang to life, infused with fresh meaning. Ginsberg now realized with a shock that those abused lines, pounded into irrelevance by overexposure, were addressing him directly, were in fact talking *about him*:

> Ah Sunflower! weary of time
> Who countest the steps of the sun;
> Seeking after the sweet golden clime,
> Where the traveller's journey is done.

While opening himself or, rather, while being opened up to this new understanding by an unknown power, Ginsberg suddenly *heard* a grave, oracular voice reciting the poem; he immediately knew it to be Blake's voice. It did not sound like any voice he recalled having heard before. It sounded "completely tender and beautifully . . . ancient. Like the voice of the Ancient of Days. . . . It was like God had a human voice with all the infinite tenderness and anciency and mortal gravity of a living Creator speaking to his son."

Intently listening to the apparitional voice, Ginsberg suddenly felt his *sight* unshuttered in a totally new way. The blue afternoon sky over East Harlem had taken on the revelatory appearance of infinite depth, allowing him to gaze at the very core of the universe: "And this was the very ancient place that he [Blake] was talking about, the sweet golden clime, I suddenly realized that *this* existence was *it!* And that I was born to experience up to this very moment . . . to realize what this was all about—in other words that this was the moment that I was born for. This initiation. Or this vision of this consciousness, of being alive unto myself, alive myself unto the Creator."

Ginsberg describes in vivid detail what it felt like to awaken or to be reborn into this new spiritual universe that felt richer and more real than anything he had experienced before. Even the old bricks and cornices of the Harlem tenements outside his window took on a new spirituality, presenting themselves as the solidification of a great deal of intelligence, as the creation of a labor of love. He began to see the evidence of spiritual labor everywhere. The sky was perceived by him as created by the living blue hand of God and even as *being* that living blue hand. He felt that God was in front of his eyes—that "existence itself was God."

Ginsberg struggles hard to convey his feeling of spiritual awe, his sense of wonder at seeing the veil of appearance lift and at being granted a glimpse of the "very secret core of the *entire* universe." Like most visionaries he is worried lest the words transmitting his vision sound inflated and hollow to the uninitiated. Hence he clings very closely to describing his immediate perception of the superreal—the sound of the ancient voice, the appearance of the cornices under the afternoon sky, the perception of the sky as the great blue hand of God.

At the signal moment of what he unquestioningly took to be a spiritual rebirth, Ginsberg felt sure that everything in the universe was vibrating toward this instant of super-consciousness: "And I felt that even my previous ponderings had been harmoniously flower-petaled toward this final understanding of what it was all about and that my poetic musings about supreme reality were prophetic, really, and just the sweet, well-intentioned strivings of a poor mind to reach what was already there."

Ginsberg was so overcome by the searing realness, the revelatory power of his visionary experience, that on the spot he made a solemn vow to himself never to forget and never to deny the apparitional voice, never to renege upon its message. Yet this spontaneous promise was broken almost in the instant of its making. Abruptly, as suddenly as it had flooded him, the mood of visionary exaltation ebbed away, to be replaced by a feeling of cold terror. What, Ginsberg asked himself, if his hearing of the Blakean voice and all that followed were just a mad delusion, the fabrication of a sick, overheated brain? What if he was going out of his mind, mistaking mental illness for superconsciousness, inflating trashy fantasies to divine messages? The fall

from the exaltation of certainty into the anxiety of doubt-
ing was devastating. No matter how hard he tried, Ginsberg
could not regain a secure foothold in the old, familiar, common-sense world out of which he had been expelled just a
few hours earlier. He tried to reassure himself by calling
himself clinical names, labeling his encounter with the
voice as "hallucinatory." Far from being presumptuous
and bold, he was willing to be reasonable and meek, to concede that he might be cracked. But in spite of his readiness
to betray his vision, he was unable to put it entirely behind
him. An indelible mark remained, rendering him unable to
resolve his vexing doubts. What, he kept wondering, if it
were all real? What "if you are born in fact into this great
cosmic universe in which you are a spirit angel—terrible
fucking situation to be confronted with. It's like being
woken up one morning by Joseph K's captors."

In order to escape from this dreadful dilemma, Ginsberg turned to others. He hoped that their reactions would
define what was real for him. If they accepted his Blakean
vision, it would gain in substance; by rejecting it, they
might help him recover his former state of innocence.
Crawling out on the fire escape, he tapped on the open
window of two girls living next door. When he told
them that he had "seen God," they banged the window
shut. Next he called an old therapist of his, telling him that
he must see him, that William Blake was in his room. The
doctor shouted "You must be crazy" and hung up. Ginsberg was not much luckier with the other people—his
father, teachers, friends—whom he tried to tell about his
cosmic vision. He ended up at the Columbia-Presbyterian
Hospital, where he stayed on the psychiatric ward for
eight months. There at least they had to listen—to some

extent. He was diagnosed as schizophrenic and meekly accepted the label. But he was deeply grateful to a young psychiatrist who, shortly before Ginsberg's discharge, had the diagnosis changed to that of extreme neurosis. It meant a great deal to Ginsberg to be thus officially certified as not insane.

One is struck by Ginsberg's sheepishness in his early brushes with official psychiatry. Besides attaching a more than administrative importance to their labeling procedures, he submissively swallowed their notions about the "unreality" of so-called hallucinations. He wanted to be a revolutionary but needed the blessing of the authorities to become one, like the Harvard freshman of the mid-sixties who said he would join Che Guevara in Bolivia if he were not worried about his mother's disapproval. For quite a while after the Blakean interlude, Ginsberg tried to make it in the conventional world by conventional means, trying his hand at market research and similar occupations. Only when he was finally given express permission by a sympathetic psychiatrist did he dare to shed his protective coloring and start doing what he had wanted to do all along: become a sort of wandering minstrel and seer of visions with a bohemian life style. But before he accepted the therapist's permission to drop out of his old, by now quite successful, life he wanted to know what the American Psychoanalytic Association would have to say about a doctor dispensing such unorthodox advice. He was told that there was no official party line.

To deny the reality of his Blakean revelation had been, for Ginsberg, an act of self-betrayal, but it was also an act of self-defense, an attempt to salvage his official sanity. Like almost every visionary's, Ginsberg's self was in danger of being swallowed up and burned to cinders by the fulgurant disclosure of the superreal. Now when he returned to it, with psychiatric sanction, he was lucky enough to find the support of a new social reality which he had helped in part to create, the "beat" and then the "hippie" scene. The counterculture served for him as a sort of cocoon within which he could function and gain prominence without landing continuously in the psychiatric ward. Also, as we shall see, it helped him to consolidate, by socializing it, the reality of his visionary experiences. He found a number of Horatios who, if they had not seen his own personal ghost, had met similar ones, with or without the aid of drugs. And nothing is as apt to make ghosts wax real and gain self-assurance as their being recognized by a whole caucus of human ghost watchers.

But before getting deeper into this topic, let us backtrack for a moment and take a closer look at the circumstances surrounding Ginsberg's first encounter with what he called Supreme Reality. At the time of the Blake vision, Ginsberg was living in almost total isolation in a dingy East Harlem tenement. His diet consisted mainly of vegetables and poems (those of others); most of his friends had left town. Shortly before the visitation by the disembodied voice he had received a jolting farewell letter from his lover, Neal Cassidy, breaking off their intense affair. This abrupt break was a severe traumatic blow for Ginsberg's brittle, lacerated self. A sort of explosive deconstriction occurred. His old reality, which had been not very solid to start with, ruptured and dissolved, and the void of his lonely agony was filled by the spectral voice, expressing infinite tenderness and love. The disintegration of his old reality had set the stage for the appearance of the supernatural which was richer and felt *more real* than anything he had experienced before. But, as we saw earlier, this superreality turned out to be unreliable, intermittent. Its eclipse threw Ginsberg into a state of nauseous suspense in which nothing seemed dependably real any more. He later described this tortured phase in the poem "The Lion for Real," where the beast is now overwhelmingly alive and now only a poor motheaten rug.

In giving a poetic contemporary form to his bliss and horror at falling off the edge of everyday reality, Ginsberg became a spokesman and figurehead for a whole coterie of spiritual desperadoes, mostly drug-propelled, who discovered and broadcast what had up to then been the secret of a few philosophers and privileged artists; what they discovered, in short, was the *relativity of reality*. What this means is that, having experienced many times, with the directness and self-evidence of immediate sensory awareness, that other realities, other modes of being, were lying hidden somewhere above or below or behind or at the periphery of everyday reality, the latter lost some of its solid robustness, of its unquestioned, safe impermeability. A reality that is no longer absolute, that can no longer claim exclusiveness with total self-assurance, unavoidably loses some of its realness. And once the monopoly of common-sense reality is questioned, we discover that far from being of one piece and uncontestable, it owes its seeming solidity and consistency to a number of artifacts, prime among which is the trick of spiriting away as "unreal" anything that does not fit.

Strictly speaking, if each man were to grow into a fullfledged individual, there would be as many realities as there are pairs of human eyes. But even the person who most fully realizes himself can never actualize all of his possibilities of being. To become an individual means precisely to exclude certain of these possibilities, to doom them to a ghostlike nonexistence. And each of these denied possibilities has as its counterpoint another possible way of appearing of the world, that is, another potential reality. The person who has been forced to bury alive too many of the possibilities belonging to him becomes haunted (neurotic or psychotic). Psychotherapy will try to help him unearth and realize some of this potential. But even those among us who pass for healthy and can get by without formal help are, in a quite precise sense, walking collective graves.

The ghosts representing our unrealized selves are uncannily persistent. Every so often they resurface—in the form of fantasies and dreams if we are fairly healthy, in the shape of "hallucinatory" materialization when a pathologically supercharged ego suffers a sudden decompression. What matters most in this encounter is how the person deals with the emergent reality, and how much of it he can appropriate for his everyday life. How well he succeeds will depend not only on his own resilience, but also on the social reality surrounding him.

To return to Ginsberg: the poet "lost" the reality disclosed to him in his Blake vision, and he felt the loss keenly. But he did not lose it totally. When the apparitional voice surged into his devastated world, he was receptive and listened closely, yet he did not surrender totally. He maintained some sense, however shaky, of his autonomy. It was this remnant of freedom which intensified his diabolical dilemma. His ego was lacerated, but not totally submerged. Being in this brittle in-between state, he could neither yield entirely to the new reality, nor resolutely re-repress it, nor actively weave it into his daily life. Instead he had to flee into the prefabricated categories of the clinic, calling himself and his vision psychiatric names.

Ginsberg was compelled, by his failure of nerve, which may have been a reflex of self-preservation, and by a lack of social support, to deny, at least provisionally, his "Supreme Reality" and to deflate it to something fictitious. In doing so, he was deflating himself. If he had been bolder and clung resolutely to his vision, he might have gone into a state of more severe and persistent psychosis, but he also might have found the way to a new, much more resilient integration. From this loftier vantage point, he might have been able to challenge the conventional distinctions between the real and the unreal, the actual and the imaginary, instead of meekly submitting to them. He might thus have entered, without the props of drugs, new worlds that were adventurous and intensely alive without being necessarily crazy or chaotic. Communicating his rich expanded surreality to sympathetic others, he would have consolidated it. And he would have discovered, much earlier than he did, that what we call unrealness is, usually, nothing but a reality which is out of place, dislocated.

Much of this Ginsberg did come to realize later, after his San Francisco therapist had given him permission to be himself and after his success as a poet and the use of drugs had emboldened him. He did not do away with the distinction between the real and the unreal altogether—a distinction which may well be one of the necessary categories of apperception in the human mind—but he redrew the borderline between the two realms in a radical manner. Thus he came to consider such tangible and seemingly powerful figures as Lyndon Johnson and Richard Nixon as mere phantoms of ghostlike insubstantiality compared to the spiritual intangibles that really mattered and which disclosed themselves, in a quasi-tangible form, in his ecstatic visions. And Ginsberg's adventures might well serve as a useful reminder that a reality which cuts itself off completely from the superreal is in danger of withering and desiccating into unrealness.

We have said that the extent to which Ginsberg could realize his vision—that is, could believe in its reality—depended ultimately on social factors beyond his control. A revelatory experience may be strictly personal and idiosyncratic at its inception, but in order to survive the always possible abortion into the merely imaginary it needs to become a reality of more than one. A purely individual reality is simply not viable.

Just imagine for a moment what the fate of Ginsberg's vision might have been if instead of being a relatively free-floating middle-class New York intellectual he had been a small-town factory worker who defined his situation in such a way that the only option open to him after his discharge from the hospital was to return to his work bench and a parental home devoid of much sympathy for anything not down to earth. In fact, I know of precisely such a case—a young worker in his twenties who went through some hallucinatory experiences not unlike those of Ginsberg—he hallucinated the presence of the sun in his darkened room. He was hospitalized for a while, and then returned to a sober, matter-of-fact workaday life, living with his well-disposed but unimaginative parents. This man did not completely deny the importance of his sun-vision, which had been tremendously meaningful to him while he experienced it. Through the support of a sympathetic psychiatrist, he was able to incorporate something of his psychotic surreality into his postpsychotic life. But given the environment to which he returned, he had to de-realize his visionary experience much more completely than Ginsberg ever did, coming to think of it as something that was "mere imagination" even though not without import.

If, on the other hand, both the hospital world and the world to which he returned after his discharge had been totally inimical to his strange experiences, if he had run up against a doctor with a straitjacket mentality who scoffed at the hallucinatory "nonsense," he probably would have been forced to forswear his sun-vision completely, deriding it not only as unreal, but also as without significance. This total recantation would have been the exorbitant price exacted for his readmission to the normal world.

Some sort of self-betrayal is the most common outcome of the visionary's struggle to salvage at least part of his hallucinatory reality for the splashdown into his workaday world. For those who manage a re-entry, it is common-sense reality which usually prevails. But its victory need not be a complete one; some fragment of the visionary experience, safely defused and encased in abstract verbiage, may be allowed to influence, from a safe distance, the conduct of the person's life.

In Ginsberg's case, the outcome was different. Ginsberg understood, however dimly, his Blakean vision, and those that followed, to portend that *something was amiss* in his world, that it had been constructed in too narrow and infantile a fashion, and that this constricted world needed to die for him to live a more adequate and human life.

It took Ginsberg some time to realize this. But in a way, in spite of his repeated lapses and his faltering wobbles, he remained loyal to his original vow and never lost sight, for very long, of the surreality which he had been allowed to behold. Instead of gradually de-realizing it, he came to accentuate its realness as he managed to find his own voice. He was able to buttress and firm it with cosmological notions which he had gleaned in his wide-ranging reading of Eastern and Western mystics. His was not a totally unprepared, empty, or passive mind. And he was lucky enough to come into his own at a juncture of American history where he could circumambulate the Pentagon in the floodlight of national publicity, chanting mantras and tinkling his finger bells, with the professed purpose of exorcising its demons—where he could do this and much more without suffering anything worse than being called names by some insufficiently exorcised bystanders.

There is no question in my mind that Ginsberg's self has been enriched by his daring to take the "unrealness" of his hallucinatory visions for real. By allowing the surreal to affect and transform his everyday life, he has undoubtedly managed to exorcise some of his personal ghosts, if not necessarily those bedeviling the nation. This does not mean that I consider Ginsberg a paragon of health or a shining emblem fit to be idolized and emulated by others. In fact, the manner in which his cosmogeny is couched, the febrile tone with which it is advanced, makes me wonder whether he has not inflated some deeper personal problem to cosmic proportions and projected it onto a firmament-sized screen rather than really having resolved it. But I am also convinced that he is far better off for having listened to, and obeyed, his Blakean voice than if he had simply, with or without psychiatric aid, stopped his ears and written off the whole experience as unreal. His case is an object lesson on the uses of psychotic daring. Like Hamlet, we might want to examine the credentials of our ghosts, to make sure we are not deceived, yet dare to take their message to heart, no matter how dubious its trappings, because to do so means to be bold enough to listen to our real self.

A second story, from a clinical source, may help illustrate the process of realizing the unreal. The struggle to appropriate a visionary experience, which presented itself in a blatantly psychotic form, was poignantly described by a young woman who was released by a schizophrenic break from the yoke of proud self-sufficiency. Unlike Ginsberg's, this woman's hallucinations were not projected out onto a cosmic screen, but led straight in to the core of her tormented personal life.

Before the onset of her liberating madness, Beatrice— as we shall call the young woman—had looked at the world in a very personal and poetic but astigmatic way. At times her vision was so acute that she could see the grass grow, at other times she was blind to the obvious. Socially poised, expert at drawing out the inarticulate, she was never at a loss for friends. But there was a touch of the peremptory in her dealings with most people which suggested to the more perceptive ones that they were dispensable. Intelligent and high-spirited, she exuded the alluringly innocent but counterfeit sensuousness of a tainted nymph which erotically sensitive men often find irresistible. She was a graduate student when she first came to clinical attention, and a number of her fellow students were wooing her without making much headway. Like Scheherezade, she was a fascinating spinner of tales who craftily postponed the yielding of herself. Physical sex, as long as it was "cool," was for her no such self-surrender. She would engage in it on occasion, with men who were safe—that is, who stood no chance of becoming important to her. She was fond of quoting Proust's words about so-called "physical possession [of a woman] where one does not possess anything."

About a year or so before her psychotic break, she found herself caught in an affair with a middle-aged man twenty years her senior. The relationship had started in an offhand way, but now, for the first time since her childhood, she felt flashes of genuine passion. "Love" had always been a dirty word to her, and she once defined the attributes of the ideal marriage as involving "separate apartments and minimum contact." And yet she found herself, inadvertently, involved with a graybeard in an affair which made her feel like a fly struggling with flypaper. Of the many roads to a woman's heart, she mused, that of the father was the most powerful. She had always been able to keep herself inviolate (her concept of love was one of mutual violation), but now Allan, her too-knowing lover, seemed to have touched the secret spring of her being. It was more than she could bear. Feeling anguished and near the point of self loss, she acted. Abruptly, without warning, with the swift, brutal brusqueness which is often the trademark of very sensitive people, she severed the affair. Allan was stunned. Unable to see her, he mailed a note: "Our affair has not died; it has been assassinated. There will be ghosts. Farewell."

Beatrice's primary reaction was relief; she felt as if she

had extricated herself from a deadly trap. Like the aging Lord Byron at the period of his Italian adventures, she remarked that she would rather drown than find herself a party to another passionate affair. She returned to her former pastime of playful, artfully managed flirtations. She marveled at a new Machiavellian discovery that even her own moods could be controlled. But about six months after the break with Allan, she sank into a state of mournful dejection which had no visible cause and seemed intractable. She would be weepy for no reason that she could understand, and obsessive thoughts, disparate strings of words, haunted her. A line of mysterious origin and obscure meaning—"O, Julius Caesar, thou are't mighty yet"—would turn and echo endlessly in her aching head. She was no longer able to sleep and quickly slipped into a psychotic state which finally led to hospitalization.

On the ward, she began to hallucinate the presence of Allan, her former lover; she heard his voice through the hot-air ducts, calling her "assassin," "murderous bitch," and other names. Slowly, reluctant to admit the grim truth, Beatrice realized that her break with Allan, seemingly consummated with neat surgical skill, had caused a deep, festering wound. For months she had given hardly a thought to her discarded lover. Now she began to yearn for him with a consuming hunger. He seemed to be oppressively present and yet as totally out of reach as if he had been whisked to another planet. Raging at herself, she read and reread his farewell letter with its somber note of finality.

After her discharge from the hospital, Beatrice sent a letter to her therapist in which she tried to sum up some of the lessons of her psychosis. In this letter, which she wrote in French, the language of her childhood, she said:

> . . . in a way I feel I came to my senses only when I was mad. The madness which I had dreaded all my life turned out to be my salvation. Only after I went crazy did I come to see the cunning deceptions perpetrated by my conscious "sane" mind with its cut-rate plastic version of reality. . . .

To accept common-sense reality as all there is, is itself a sign of insanity. This official reality, noteworthy for the myriad of things it ignores, now strikes me as a *"folie à millions,"* a collective madness. No democratic nose count, no consensus exceeding the dreams of the wiliest politician, can freeze reality and decree its ultimate nature. What is real, after all? What affects me. Nothing has affected me more deeply, nothing has been more real, than my visions in that hospital. The voices I heard there shook me to the roots of my being; their echoes, hardly muffled by time, still rule my present life.

If my so-called madness had taught me nothing but to distrust the stratagems of my conscious mind, its lesson would have been invaluable. I had to fall ill to see the hollowness and deformity of my most basic beliefs. I had to proceed slyly, by subterfuge, to find out what was really on my mind. Often it paid to stand a conscious thought on its head. In fact, had I turned all my conscious thoughts inside out, one by one, I would have been closer to the truth of my feelings, most of the time, than by taking them, naïvely, at face value. After I had been in the hospital a few weeks, I started a therapy hour with the remark: "I have not been thinking of Bob [a psychiatric aide] of late; this must mean that he is on my mind." This seemingly perverse sophism led me straight to an important truth.

Or take my break with Allan, my too-earthy lover. After cutting loose from him, I was soaring. But I failed to realize the dizziness of my flight; I ignored that Allan had grounded me in more than one sense. Chafing under his weight, I forgot that this very weight had anchored me. To bid farewell to Allan seemed a great relief. For six months I managed to deceive myself, until my delusional state finally brought me face to face with the truth. Only when I saw Allan's luminous eyes stare at me from the faces of grayish ward attendants, when I heard his cracked voice coming at me from the hospital's air ducts, when I screamed with terror because I was sure that a doctor who had stolen Allan's features was going to wrench my bloody heart out of my living body—only then did it dawn on me that the loss of Allan was unbearable. Crouched in a corner, shrinking from any human presence, my face drenched with tears, I suddenly recalled the line of a poet I had read many years ago without taking it in. His words, which had been patiently biding their time to be resurrected in a mind lacerated and made supple by sorrow, said that every parting from a loved person, if it were experienced fully, would lead straight to madness. And realizing this, I understood, at last, the meaning of the haunting refrain which had been with me for days: "O, Julius Caesar, thou are't mighty yet." Of course, these were the words by which Shakespeare's Brutus acknowledges the triumphant presence of the slain dictator. Like the Roman soldier, I was pursued by a ghost, the ghost of the dear assassinated one.

My grieving at Allan's loss brought back to life, with startling freshness, a distant past long consigned to oblivion. I had always deplored the sterility of my memory, which refused to yield up any events of my early childhood. Now the death of my grandfather, when I was barely two, came back to me with such vivid detail, with a concreteness of sights, sounds, and smells as if it was taking place right then. For a while, the distinction between past and present became blurred. I relived the departure of Anna, my Negro nanny with the large cuddly breasts, who was sent away for mysterious reasons when I was three. These surfacing images were bound together and sustained by an identity of mood, a sense of irreparable loss. By opening myself to my sorrow, I had reclaimed part of my lost history. I felt as if released from the bondage of time. For all I knew, time—at least, the homogenized time doled out by our clocks—was just another invention of anxiety, an astringent frame we use to tame raw reality.

But if time in fact, as my psychotic experience led me to believe, was not homogeneous and irreversible but could in mysterious ways return upon itself, then perhaps there was no such thing as a final loss, then perhaps my psychotic certainty that Allan and my dead grandfather were still present need not have been deluded. The paradoxical happened: while I was feverishly hallucinating the presence of Allan and at the same time tearfully mourning his irretrievable loss [while Beatrice was in the hospital, Allan married another woman], I came to feel that the tie between us had not been dissolved, was, in fact, indissoluble. Perhaps the views of the Catholic Church on the permanence of the marriage bond are based on a psychological insight of this sort. If I was only bold enough to take my so-called delusion seriously, not to be cowed by the prissy dictates of common sense, then perhaps I could keep in touch with that surreality grounding everyday reality (and surrounding it on all sides) of which I had caught glimpses during my psychotic state.

Once I had boldly decided that we need not bow to the pressure of everyday reality, many things fell into place. I thought of those Jews at Auschwitz who had gone to the gas chamber in the belief that no evil could befall them because they were protected by a higher power. Sure, from a mundane point of view this faith in the inviolability of their fate was tragically deluded. And yet only the narrowly earthbound will fail to wonder whether, in some ultimate sense, these pitiful victims, about to go up in smoke, may not have been right, and whether their blind, stubborn faith had not transported them, before their physical extinction, to regions from where the tears of those weeping for them were oddly irrelevant.

When I first met you [the therapist], I told you that more than anything else I wanted you to give me courage, courage not to turn my back on the scary apparitions rising from the ruins of my old, cracked world. I needed your help to make them endure. Now

I am busy translating my psychotic insights into plain language so that I can embody them in my daily life. In this process of translation, some of the lustrous immediacy of my original visions is bound to fade, but what is proof against fading, I trust, is the faith in the realness and unbounded richness of the surreality from which the limited shapes of our sensible reality spring and into which, used up, they sink back, to be replaced by others waiting their turn to be unveiled.

Here ends the letter of Beatrice who "came only to her senses when she went mad." At no time has Beatrice played down the terror she felt when she saw her formerly solid world dissolve before her eyes, watched reality turn into something fluid and relative, something that allowed of more or less, which could wax or wane abruptly like images in a horror show. Even though she did not have any choice in the matter, she did not doubt for a moment that the anguish she endured when her old brittle world collapsed had been worthwhile. When she finally fell into the abyss she had been afraid of all her life, she was not smashed to pieces and did not die. What died was only an old, outworn way of living, a fossilized reality which she had mistaken for the totality of her self.

Beatrice's friends agree that she has come out of her harrowing experience a much more complete and open person. She has lost some of the sharp angularity which kept others at bay and injured them when they ventured too close. Without losing any of her individuality, she has become more accommodating. The idea of marriage no longer seems totally absurd to her. And she realizes that in certain respects she remains more fragile than her more robust friends who grew straight from the beginning and did not have to go through a traumatic second birth.

The relatively happy outcome of the psychotic episodes of Beatrice and Ginsberg is not very common in our society, whose members have become inured to the uncanniness of modern technology but respond with instinctive anxiety whenever the uncanny intrudes in a more old-fashioned, ghostlike way. Hence there is strong social pressure, of which psychiatrists are the more or less naïve agents, for the psychotic to forswear his heresy and to deny the reality of what he has experienced.

Without falsely romanticizing madness, it is obvious that in many psychotic states a deep psychic truth breaks through. What is tragic is not that the average madman believes in his delusions, but that he does not believe *enough* in them. By timidly averting his eyes from the realness of the unreal which wants to disclose itself to him, he loses his chance at self-realization.

It shows great myopia to see only the catastrophic shipwreck of a human life that madness may portend. On the face of it, psychotic states are often characterized, especially in their initial phases, by a tremendous richness of inner experience, by the tapping of vast psychic powers; in comparison the normal state, not only of the prepsychotic but of most healthy people, appears paltry and vapid.

In fact, psychosis holds a lesson for all of us in that it can make us aware of the indigence and bankruptcy of the norms of mental health by which our society lives. Psychosis, in other words, reveals the ghostlike unreality and impoverishment of the inner lives of many who have nothing to do with madness, who will never go out of

37

their minds, who may even pass for models of healthiness, and who yet, by the standard of their own potential, are but poor impersonators of their real self.

It is ironic and sad that quite a few of the more fervent worshipers of the gospel of normality are plagued by the (almost always unfounded) fear that they might one day lose their mind. If they are asked to define this fear, as a rule they cannot, and have only vague notions of what going crazy would involve in their case. If they are pressed further it invariably turns out that the state they fear most (the state of being mad) represents for them the state in which their deepest wishes and yearnings, which they hardly dare admit to themselves, would surface and, perhaps, be partly fulfilled. Thus madness could be, for these prisoners of normality, a blessed release, as physical illness sometimes is, a condition to be wished for as much as feared. But they have lost the boldness to want what they wish.

The lesson of cases like Ginsberg's and Beatrice's is not that everybody ought to be psychotic at least once in a lifetime, as some contemporary authors, eulogizing their own psychoses, seem to suggest. Madness is not available to everyone. The lesson is rather that when our everyday reality becomes so shopworn and threadbare that it ceases to nourish us, we have to accept the real in whatever outlandish shape it may adopt. For the psychotic, this means accepting the realness of his hallucinatory unreality. For the less impoverished neurotic it means, as we shall see in the next chapter, rediscovering the realness of his dreams.

2

DREAMS

The Radiant Children
of the Night

We have dealt in the first chapter with the person who, in broad daylight, sees his familiar reality crumble, sees it replaced by an alien surreality extruded by his deepest, his innermost self. It tells us little, in fact it may be mostly misleading, if we label such a mode of experience as psychotic.

The person who hears "imaginary" voices and who has "visions" has stumbled upon a denied, disavowed reality which seizes and overpowers him. But how about the average person whose daylight reality is safe from the intrusions of the uncanny? He, too, in order to become who he is had to deny certain possibilities of being. He, too, in order to create the coherence of a real world, had to banish a great many experiences, actual or potential, as "unreal."

But no matter how solidly he seems installed in the fortress of his everyday world, he will never be totally safe. The denied ghosts of the past, the condemned promises of the future, will not leave him alone. If he manages to ignore their hovering presence in the alert state of waking, they will take possession of him, under the cover of night, in the state of unprotectedness which we call sleep. They will do so in the guise of dreams. Tentative and evanescent, less overpowering than the visitations of the so-called psychotic, these nighttime visitors tend to vanish at the approach of wakefulness. They concede to the dreamer a margin of freedom (including the freedom of ignoring them) which the psychotic no longer possesses. But in spite of their shadowy discreetness, their readiness to take flight when challenged, they can be terribly persistent. The dream, we might say, is the collapsible but indestructible domain of unreality in which the denied reality of the average person manifests itself.

Whatever the particular language used—whether the dream is called "a messenger from the gods" or "the royal road to the unconscious"—it has been recognized, since the dawn of prehistory, as giving man access to an order of reality which transcends and may not mesh with the reality of his everyday world. But as for the reality of the dream itself, the respect paid to it has been intermittent. Some cultures, during certain periods of their history, have had little use for dreams. There are ways of defining reality which are more impervious to the claims of the dream adventure than others. Thus it was one of the merits of Sigmund Freud to have rescued the dream from the disrepute into which it had fallen among his positivistic contemporaries. Yet, as we shall see, Freud's rehabilitation of the dream was only a partial one.

Let us look, for a moment, at the Freudian attempt to re-
define reality in such a way as to clear a space for the
reality of the dream. (Freud considered *Interpretation of
Dreams* his most important book. Hence he was not surprised that for decades nobody read it.) In essence, Freud
saw the dream as a major bridge between the newly promul-
gated reality of the unconscious and the old reality of consciousness. He stripped it of most of the prophetic, divina-
tory aspects which had loomed large in the romantic era
preceding his period. He tried to make the willful "children
of the night" palatable to his dubious contemporaries by
forcing them to submit to the discipline of intellectual
analysis. He strove to prove that their playful, teasing poetry
could be made to yield rigorous precise meanings.

All along, one senses a marked unease in Freud's dealings
with these compromising, libidinous creatures of the dark.
His tone is defensive, at times apologetic. His lack of ease
leads him to make dubious sweeping assumptions about the
wish-fulfilling nature of all dreams. He accuses the dream
of deceptiveness, of hiding its real intentions, its "latent
thoughts," behind the "façade" of the manifest dream (i.e.,
the dream as actually dreamed). This "justifies" him in the
rather high-handed, arbitrary measures he uses in dealing
with the actual dream.

Freud did not go the whole way in reinstating the reality
of the dream. He did not allow it to challenge the arrogant
claim to pre-eminence of the waking world. The thought
hardly occurred to him. He claimed for the dream the
status of being "psychologically" real, but it was axiomatic
for him that this merely psychological reality was less sub-
stantial, less real than the robust reality of waking.

Freud's handling of the dream is decidedly ungentle.
Starting from the premise that the dream is a master of

deception, he tears apart its web, fragmenting and pulverizing it. Deeply suspicious, he is most afraid of being taken in. His glance fastens, Sherlock Holmes style, upon tiny, seemingly trivial details, by means of which he hopes to detect the suspect's hidden workings. These microscopic clues are to be woven, with the aid of free association, into a tight net of circumstantial evidence which will convince the most finicky jury.

Freud is particularly impatient with the dream's charade of disguising itself by means of symbols. He rips these symbolic masks off so energetically that he hardly notices how his vehemence denudes the dream and reduces it to an amorphous pulp, unable to resist his most arbitrary interpretations. In other words, the dream is treated by Freud as a hardened criminal who must be subjected to the third degree. Only thus can its secret be torn from it. One is reminded of Karl Jaspers' comment about the "police mentality" of psychoanalysis.

Is such toughness really called for in dealing with the gossamer stuff of dreams? One does not make butterflies talk by tearing off their wings. Can we not do without this Freudian machinery of hostile interrogation? What if we approached the dream gently, respecting its integrity, treating it courteously, as we might an honored visitor from abroad? We might then discover that the dream will talk to us of its own volition and that some of its obscurity will fade away.

A large part of the enigmatic nature of dreams is an artifact of the dreamer's or the would-be interpreter's anxiousness. It is the mind trying to read the dream which infects it with its own opaqueness. The dreamer himself may be unfit to get at his dream's core for the same reason that a person cannot see his own blind spot. The professional interpreter of dreams, the therapist, on the other hand, may be blinded by his theorizing, which has taught him to silence unbidden voices by obfuscation. What is needed more than anything else to understand the gesturing of the dream is an almost childlike, incorruptible simplicity which is not taken in by contrived complexities and is able to see, in the midst of them—the obvious. Such simple-mindedness is, among clinicians, a very rare commodity. Once lost, it is almost impossible to recover. Thus a compulsive person dreaming about a crab may torture himself to establish the meaning of his dream by means of symbolic equivalences and elaborate associations. But perhaps the most valuable message of the dream for him was something as obvious—and yet totally hidden from him—as his being "crabbed." Or perhaps the dream meant to convey to him that the whole movement of his life was retrograde, that like the legendary crab he was "walking backward." Such simple-minded readings often have the most profound effect upon people lost in their labyrinthine intricacies, whose dreams seem to mirror the convolutedness of their lives, for whom, in short, "complexity" is a major mode of defense. Nothing is more beyond the grasp of such unfortunates, and nothing is more salutary to them, than the naïve simplicity which uncovers meaningful patterns in the chaotically confused tracings of their lives. (As we shall see, simplicity, which at times may look like simple-mindedness, is an essential requirement not only for the reader of dreams, but also for the good therapist.)

Let it be said in passing that most dreams which emerge while a person is in therapy may be looked at as collaborative ventures. They are co-produced, as it were, by the patient and his therapist. It is well known that people who go to psychoanalysts dream Freudian dreams, and that those who go to Jungians dream about mandalas. My own patients humor me by producing a large proportion of dreams which have the limpidity of unpretentious poetry. The communications of such dreams are often peculiarly compelling.

Sometimes, the language of the dream is so transparent, its imagery so direct that hardly any translation is needed. Such was the dream of a neurotic patient in his late twenties who dreamed of a torture laboratory disguised as a pleasure yacht. He was aboard with a former girlfriend. Also present was a little boy with silver braces on his legs who sang plaintive songs about ideal love. The patient tells the girl that something is wrong with the ship. He is overheard through a vent. Suddenly the master of the yacht turns on a vacuum mechanism with a tremendous sucking power which swallows people. The patient manages to escape, but his companion is sucked in and tortured. Transfixed, he listens to her moans, which are like cries of lust during the sexual act.

This dream could be read as an artfully condensed biography of the patient, who, even though gloomy and depressed, had always maintained that most of his life, including his childhood, had been a pleasure trip. In spite of its forwardness, the dream initially failed to register with him. He could not do anything with it; it seemed irrelevant, disconnected from the present context of his life. He was ready to dismiss it when I intervened. Adopting a low-profile stance, I asked him quietly, but repeatedly, whether he could really not relate the torture yacht to anything in his life. He asked me if I could. My answer was affirmative.

After a long silence, he allowed that he had some wild, far-out idea that he once took a boat trip with his family. The outing had been billed as a happy treat and he had managed to experience it as such, but at bottom it had been a nightmarish disaster. He was not sure, though—in fact, he doubted—that such a trip had ever actually taken place. "Never mind," I told him, "just let us hear more about it." Slowly, very slowly, some details began to emerge, and even more slowly it began to dawn on him that the dream might have a much deeper import. For the first time, he began to question whether the recollected lost paradise of his childhood had been more than a myth. The dream which ten minutes earlier had appeared irrelevant now took on the lineaments of an uncannily apt revelation. Perhaps his lost childhood Eden had been, in actuality, a camouflaged torture lab. Perhaps he himself had been dwarfed and crippled, reduced to crooning wistful songs about ideal love, while those who pretended to love and protect him had been man-eating vacuum machines which had devoured parts of his self. The dream, to become real enough to puncture the lifelong pseudo-reality of the pleasure trip, needed to be sustained by somebody outside of the dreamer (in this case, the therapist). The impact upon the patient was shattering.

Some time later, the same patient had a fairy-tale dream which was slightly more disguised (it occurred during a period of heightened defensiveness), but which again did not require much pulling and squeezing to reveal a meaning. The dream was about a dog which turned into a horse that wanted to walk on its hind legs. The patient wanted to force the horse to walk on all fours. The horse tried, but managed only a pathetic crawl. Finally the patient relented and let the horse walk on its hind legs like a human, where-upon it turned into a very attractive woman.

Here we see the patient embattled, struggling to become human. But the old habits of cruelty, contracted on the torture yacht, die hard. Only when he desists from his self-rape and gives his animal side its head, no matter how "unnatural" its aspirations, can he finally transcend it and grow into a human being. (In exact correspondence to the patient's as yet undeveloped maleness, it was a young *woman* who emerged from the dog-changed-into-horse. In later dreams of his, this young woman evolved—*pace* Women's Lib!—into a man.) Again, the dream needed to be legitimized by the therapist in order to become real for the patient; once "realized" in this way, it affected him deeply.

Sometimes dreams are even more concise in making their statement. Thus a patient dreamed that he had stopped coming to therapy but continued paying his bills for the sessions. We made the mistake of not heeding the dream. After all, the patient was appearing regularly for his appointments. Only later, in retrospect, did I realize that the dream had been right: while the patient was physically present, he was not really "there" during the hour. A couple of weeks after the unheeded dream, another dream gave an even broader hint. The patient dreamed that I told him I "could not hack it any more" with him. This dream made *me* realize how weary I was of this very demanding patient whom I had been seeing for a number of years.

And here is one more example of a simple dream simply explicated. A middle-aged man dreams he is in another part of his hometown, far away on a hill on the other side. It is a gray twilight, slightly chill. His daughter tells him, as she goes off down the hill, that she will be back and that meanwhile he is to get his Christmas tree planted by the time she returns. It is not a very good tree, though already decorated in traditional style. The ground there is flinty; the father has no adequate shovel; there will be little time. He cannot possibly manage. Meanwhile, he is expected elsewhere to do another assignment, and has a vague, uneasy awareness of yet a third place he "should" be. This feels all too familiar to him. He awakes still "in" the dream and it is some time before he can stop feeling helplessly hopeless.

This is, indeed, a simple dream, for it states quite directly the story of his life. The patient's earliest memories are of being told how inept he was at the simplest tasks (painting a wall, for example), and his current situation is one in which he often finds himself double- and triple-appointed at the same hour, each appointment representing a task for which he must function well above the top of his bent. His daughter presents him with the immediate problem of making more money than he has ever been able to make in order to pay for her college. In his hometown he was regarded as a harmless social incompetent who had ten thumbs. In short, the dream neatly states a half century of his being in the world. It is what one calls a "spotlight fantasy."

It is also a dream that readily admits of technical Freudian manipulation. All the standard images it contains (Christmas tree, inadequate shovel, flinty ground, hill) could be translated just as the sexual symbols the *Traumdeutung* says they should be. For this man, sex had been a source of "examination anxiety" quite along orthodox theoretical lines. However, sex was, for him, but one in a list that lengthened without limit of baffling, ill-specified, unreasonably complicated demands put upon him simultaneously and then defined into insolubility by a succession of women. It was merely one part of his lifelong stress overload.

The two uses of this one dream are instructive here. Both are "valid" interpretations. The first is less of an "interpretation" than the second, and much more general. The Freudian manipulation derives by cryptography only one of myriad examples of the existential condition of this man that the dream very directly states.

Not all dreams are as limpid as the dreams just cited. Even my patients have dreams which impress both them and me as opaque, and which do not readily yield a plausible meaning. Perhaps these dreams are recalcitrant because, for whatever reason, I am not sufficiently attuned to them. However, there they are. If the dream is convoluted in addition to being enigmatic, I may be able to salvage something by lifting a relatively lucid part out of it; this is a case of outwitting the dream by treating it as more communicative than it really is. But usually I prefer to simply ignore dreams which put on airs. I realize that by going to a lot of trouble I could probably extract from them some sort of message. But is it a message worth getting? I am convinced that the intricate interpretations in which Freudian dream exegesis delights are, as a rule, of little therapeutic benefit. Some reality may shine even through such clever explanations but it is too diluted to have much of an effect. (At any rate, the therapist dealing with the dream life of his patients always faces a problem of selection. He might as well favor those dreams which promise the richest therapeutic yield.)

Once in a while a person has a dream which seems to him of earth-shaking importance while he dreams it but upon awakening seems flat and trivial, if not senseless. The sober light of day seems to have revealed that he was taken in by the black magic of the night. But this conclusion is premature.

What actually happens is that the dreamer, upon awakening, re-enters the reality of his daylight world which is governed by laws quite different from those which rule his sleeptime happenings. The two orders of reality, waking reality and dream reality, are largely incommensurable, especially in the case of the person who lives in a neurotically constricted universe. The awakened dreamer usually accepts without question—unless he happens to be a poet or a philosopher—the claim of daylight reality to exclusive legitimacy. In so doing, he dooms the differently constituted reality of the night to crumble into ghostlike unrealness. What had sparkled like a precious jewel in the fluorescent shimmer of the night turns, in the glare of day, into worthless trash.

But, contrary to what the awakened dreamer thinks, the daylight perspective need not prevail. His nighttime faith in having found a treasure need not have been deluded. In fact, the reality of the dream, and the often far from trivial truth it tried to convey, can, as a rule, be retrieved quite easily in the setting of therapy. If this truth has been eclipsed, it is because the awakened dreamer was too timorous to sustain it. All it takes to recover it is the therapist's determination to support the dream realm against the overbearing, exclusive rationality of the daylight world. One could say that the dusklike "unreality" of the therapeutic situation beckons the reality of the dream to re-emerge.

A case in point is the story of a patient who dreamed that his wife's breast had a very elongated, trunklike nipple which looked like an erect penis. While asleep, the patient was sure that this dream was somehow very significant. But upon awakening, he found it merely silly. Later in the day, he told me about his "foolish" dream. When I wondered aloud, a couple of times, whether the dream was indeed as foolish as he said, he turned thoughtful. He had been wondering that morning, he said, what it might mean when people brand an event they have experienced as unreal; did it really matter much whether they were awake or asleep, sober or drugged, alert or somnolent, while undergoing the experience? Perhaps calling something unreal was only a way of asking it to go away. Knowing his penchant for philosophical generalities, I asked him to be more concrete. He fell silent, then his face lighted up. "I think I know now what the dream was all about," he said. "It has made me understand why I have been shrinking all my life from concrete reality. The dream told me that Reality is my mother's breast raping me."

It turned out that this insight was very pregnant for the patient. It illuminated, in a flash, many of his ways of behaving which, up to then, had been mysterious to him. It shed light on his habit of fleeing compulsively into intellectual abstractions (his field of study was mathematical logic). More importantly, it explained why this man, who by his whole stance and demeanor always seemed to ask those he came into contact with to give something to him, was unable to accept the gifts that were proffered. All gifts were irredeemably poisoned for him because the original gift, his mother's milk, had been thrust upon him in a sadistic way. That is why he had to keep the seemingly most benevolent figures at double arm's length. Realizing for the first time how starved he had been all his life while suffering the agonies of Tantalus, he wept bittersweet tears in which sorrow mingled with relief. He felt that perhaps now he would no longer have to reject all tokens of love. And indeed he became more open and accepting. The almost discarded gift of the dream enabled him to negotiate a major turning point.

This patient had long been dubious that dreams had anything real to offer. But at the same time he would mention on occasion—as many neurotics do—that in his dreams he experienced events much more vividly, felt much more involved and awake, than in his dull, sleepy waking life. In fact, many of his dream experiences grabbed him with an immediacy which he wished for but could not attain during his waking hours. While in the midst of these nightly happenings, it did not occur to him to question their reality. That happened only as he woke up or came close to awakening. Only then, to regain a hold of his brittle, thinly textured daylight reality, would he tell himself that it was "only a dream."

(The fact that neurotics who lead impoverished lives often dream richly has its counterpart in the plaint of a poet friend of mine that his daily life was so abundant that there was not much left for his dreams. He tried to come to terms with the relative poverty of his dreams by formulating a general law according to which the richness of a person's dream life is in proportion to the poverty of his waking life. But it is a miserable business to try to formulate general laws in psychology; the published dreams of writers who led rich and active lives seem to invalidate my friend's self-protective thesis.)

In order to allow the dream its fullest scope, it is important for us to move beyond the Freudian recognition of the dream as *"psychologically"* real and to accept it as *really real*. In other words, we need to refrain from prejudging the realness of the dream. If we do this, the dream will affect us much more deeply.

It was the late Fritz Perls who, borrowing heavily from the dream theories of C. G. Jung and others, popularized some of the techniques of resurrecting the dream to full-fledged actuality. This sort of endeavor, incidentally, seems to be "in the air," promoted by the Zeitgeist. It crops up in many places, among Jungians, existentialists, Gestaltists, primal therapists, adherents of the encounter cult. Is it, perhaps, that to the extent that our collective everyday lives are emptied of substance we are driven to attempt to recover the lost reality in the realm of the dream?

One of Perls's major technical devices is to require the person to report his dream in the present tense. Thus if somebody begins to tell his dream by saying "I was walking along the road when I saw," he is stopped and asked to begin again in this way: "I am walking along a road and I see . . ." This simple shift makes a vast difference experientially, and the person may be encouraged to "act out" his dream, not only playing various dream personages but impersonating objects and even localities of the dream. He is told to ham it up, to make things as real as possible.

If the dreamer does this—if, for instance, he becomes the dream trail he had been walking on, by saying "I am a trail. People walk on me. I am brown and muddy," etc.— the dream takes on a vivid reality. Forgotten dream details re-emerge with a startling sharpness of perceptual detail. As the person involves himself with the people and objects of his dream, powerful affects may be released which the person was incapable of feeling in his waking life. Sometimes a dreamer will be asked to bring to its logical conclusion a dream cut short by anxiety. Thus Perls reports the story of a man named Chuck who several times had the same nightmare in which his little boy ran in front of his car and was about to be hit by him. At this point Chuck would wake up, very frightened. Perls asked him to pursue the dream to its end—that is, to kill his son, and then talk to the dead boy.

In acting out this scene, Chuck became very agitated. He began to cry, voicing deep sadness about having wronged his son: "I'm sorry that I pushed you away—all the times I pushed you away when I was doing something that . . . I felt was very important to me—and the really important thing was not what I was doing but the fact that you wanted to—be with Daddy."

These various techniques of recovering and amplifying the reality of dreams may have the effect of making the dreamer doubt the reality of his daylight world. If it is brittle, it may shatter. He must then use parts of his nighttime universe to build a more shatterproof waking world.

Once we have decided to take the dream seriously, once we begin to question the claim of the daylight world to be the uncontested arbiter of what is real, we are faced by a new perplexity which at the same time is a very old philosophic riddle. Once we are in earnest about letting the phenomena of the dream appear undimmed, without prejudging them by the categories of awakeness, we are ineluctably led to ask: if the dream world appears as real to us while we are dreaming as the waking world does while we are awake, what makes us decide that the one reality is more valid than the other? If dream experiences are invested with the same stamp of reality that waking experiences are, how can we be sure that the world of our awakeness is not just another dream? Are there criteria which allow us to distinguish reliably between waking and dreaming? These riddles are as old as the history of Eastern and Western philosophy, but, as Hannah Arendt has pointed out, they have taken on a haunting urgency for Western thinkers since the philosophical revolution set in motion by René Descartes.

By elevating doubt to be the first principle of philosophy, Descartes prepared the foundation of modern science, a science based, according to Karl Marx, upon the assumption that Being and Appearance have parted company forever. At the historical jucture when Western man began to lose faith in the trustworthiness of his senses, he began to question the realness of what presented itself as reality. As is often the case, there was a vast cultural lag. It took a few centuries for the bad news to filter down from the philosophers to the middle-brow neurotics who themselves often are trend-setters for tomorrow's ruling style of general consciousness. Half a century ago, Freud's neurotics, by and large, hardly ever doubted that they were real; they were people who felt solidly planted in a real world but to whom funny things kept happening. Descartes's radical doubt, in its coarsened Kafkaesque form, has only recently become endemic among the various types of neurotics who worry about the dislocation, or the intermittence, of their sense of reality.

Descartes, in his *Meditations*, says that he cannot be sure whether he is asleep or awake. Starting from the premise that "all the same thoughts and conceptions which we have while awake may also come to us in sleep," he concludes that "there are no certain indications by which we may clearly distinguish wakefulness from sleep." Descartes illustrated his perplexity about the relation between the two orders of reality by a parable. Let us suppose, he said, that there was a man who had continuous coherent dreams and who, while dreaming, was transported to various dissimilar places; waking up each time in a new environment, without links to the preceding place and the one to follow, would not this man find the world of his dreams more real than the intermittent, kaleidoscopic world which would greet him upon awakening?

Descartes's theme was taken up in a literary form by his contemporary Calderon. In the play *Life Is a Dream* Calderon tells the story of an imprisoned prince, Sigismond, who is carried, while drugged, from his jail to the royal palace. There he wakes up, sumptuously dressed, and, by order of the king, is treated as if he were the sovereign. Sigismond at first wonders whether he is not dreaming; then, deciding that his situation is real, he quickly shows himself a brutal tyrant. Drugged again, he is whisked back to jail. When he wakes up in his old rags, he is easily persuaded that the interlude in the palace was but a dream. Sometime later he is set free and becomes the real king, but by then he is sure that these curious happenings are merely fragments of a dream. The two orders, the realm of waking and that of dreaming, have been confounded for him irredeemably.

Now when Descartes wondered whether he was dreaming or awake, his point was not that while in the state we call waking we have no empirical criteria by which we can distinguish between waking and dreaming, but that while dreaming we are unaware of the existence of the other, waking, reality and are hence deluded. Now how can we be sure, Descartes muses, that our waking experiences are not equally delusions, concocted by an *"esprit trompeur,"* an evil spirit who plays games with man?

The answer is that there is no such certainty. Once we begin to search for an Archimedean point located outside of both waking and dreaming reality, the distinctions between real and unreal become fuzzy indeed. But if we are less ambitious and content ourselves to remain within the sphere circumscribed by the two realities, we may be able to deepen our understanding of both by examining, more thoroughly, their differences and their dynamic interplay.

Now the main distinction usually made between waking and dreaming is the following: waking reality is coherent, continuous, and relatively permanent whereas dream reality is flighty, kaleidoscopic, ephemeral. The figures and objects in the dream are subject to magical changes, sudden Ovidian metamorphoses—like the one of dog into horse into beautiful woman in the dream described earlier. These transformations do not come about gradually, as they would in waking life; the dreamer is always confronted by the *fait accompli* of dog-become-horse.

Waking reality does not tolerate such capricious leaps. Within its confines, the friend of mine who died yesterday will still be reliably dead tomorrow, whereas in the dream the corpse of a moment ago may be fully alive the next instant. But, as Ludwig Klages has pointed out, this dependability of the waking world is contingent upon a subjective factor, the continuity of our memory. It is our memory which guarantees that we experience the room in which we wake up as the same in which we went to sleep the night before (even if some furniture has been moved around while we slept). If the bonds of memory which tie our waking experiences together were to lapse, we would wake up each morning, without having displaced ourselves, in totally new, unfamiliar places.

Something of this kind is precisely what happens in dreams. I may dream the same dream over and over again, as happens with recurring nightmares, without being aware, while dreaming, that I am repeating an earlier dream (Klages talks about the *"jamais vu"* of the dream), or my dream of tonight may pick up a theme adumbrated in last night's dream without my knowing that this is happening. The dream, in other words, resembles a movie whose frames do not know of each other. Only two options exist: either the same frame is exposed again, or there is a sudden leap. In order to bridge the discontinuities of the dream, to connect parts of dreams or several dreams with each other, something external to the dream must be brought to bear: the conscious awareness of a person who is awake.

Only the awake person can understand the dream, which means that no dream, no matter how limpid in appearance, is wholly self-explanatory; waking consciousness is bound to come into play. Hence there is always a margin of freedom, always more than one possible reading. It is only the synthesis of dream experience (as refracted by memory) and conscious explication which fully *realizes* the dream. The weaving of the dream into the fabric of our waking consciousness is an integral part of the reality of dreaming.

The fact that even the simplest dream cannot stand by itself, as it were, is illustrated by a story about Socrates' dream life related in *Phaidon*. According to this story, Socrates began to write poetry during the last days of his life in jail. He did so, he explained to a friend, because of a recurring dream which told him, with slight variations, that he ought to serve the muses. For a long time, Socrates thought that this dream meant to encourage him to continue what he was already doing. After all, he reasoned, to be a philosopher meant to pursue the noblest of arts. But while he was in prison, it occurred to him that the dream might be read quite differently. Perhaps rather than exhorting him to persist in his quest for rational knowledge, it meant to point out a deficiency in his way of life. Perhaps it was admonishing him to serve the muses more directly and to develop his neglected poetical side. Socrates felt that he would be more at peace if he obeyed this injunction. Hence on the threshold of death he turned poet and wrote a hymn in praise of the god whose feast was then being celebrated. (We might mention, in passing, that this story of Socrates also favors our thesis about the desirability of directness and simplicity in the reading of dreams. Socrates' first explication was intellectualized and thus too complex.)

Socrates thought of his dream as a message from the gods. Modern man may not think in these terms, but there is nothing which compels us to consider dream reality as deficient relative to waking reality. Different, to be sure, but not necessarily less real. For all we know, the dream, like the hallucinatory vision, may give us access to a surreality which is beyond man's ken during his usual waking state, but which he ignores at his own peril. Perhaps the dream is, for the average man dazed by the buzzing clatter of our speeded-up world, the last natural channel of communication with his own depth—and with the supernatural. Perhaps the reality of my dream which presents the friend who died yesterday as being alive expresses a more essential truth than the limited daylight view which bows before the finality of the "fact" of death.

Perhaps also, by paying close attention to the nature of our dream reality, we may be enabled to discover features of our waking world which usually escape notice. Perhaps our waking world is, in some ways, much more jumpy and discontinuous, more "dreamlike," than we ordinarily realize. It is possible that its gaps and interstices are merely being papered over by the incessant collating and editing operations of our conscious mind. If we take the notion seriously—which much clinical material seems to substantiate—that our (prerational) emotions are what connects us most immediately with our experienced world, and if we keep in mind the vagaries, the sudden ups and downs, of our emotional voltage, then we might come to wonder whether the fluctuating, intermittent mode of experiencing of our dreams does not give a more accurate picture of our engagements with reality than the false smoothness displayed by the hand-me-down reality of common sense.

More important still: by confining us in hermetic seclusion, by sequestering us in an isolation which is almost absolute—a dream can be reported after the fact, but it cannot actually be shared—the dream individualizes and condenses our private world to the utmost, tears away the veils of false certainties and brings us face to face, at last, with the ghostlike truth which, while awake, we had managed to evade. Many a person who goes to sleep believing that he is deeply in love, discovers while dreaming that he was mistaken—a discovery often pushed aside at the break of day, only to be ruefully remembered much later. In light of the clairvoyant acuity of the dream, waking reality is exposed as an aggregate of shadowy, obtuse, and deceptive appearances.

But the dream, for all its luminous power, cannot substitute for waking experience. It can illuminate, but it cannot *make* history. The neglected existential tasks pinpointed by the dream need to be taken up in daily life. This is sometimes overlooked by neurotics who, having discovered the treasure trove of dreams, spend their time waiting for dreams to do their life work for them; they are invariably disappointed.

Dream experience and waking experience are not symmetrical; one is incomplete without the other. A person who spent all his life dreaming would keep dreaming the same dreams. He might have a series of disjointed experiences, but not a true history. The person who led a dreamless life, who ignored the realm of the dream, would be, in an important sense, only partly awake. His life would be deficient in depth and scope; it would not be completely real.

A psychotherapy in pursuit of realness will have to restore the reality of the dream for those who lead dreamforsaken lives.

3

VIOLENCE

The Attempted Breakthrough

The person who is walled in by his unreality, and who is too much out of touch with his dreams to work his way gradually to freedom, may resort to desperate expedients to reassure himself that he is real.

Foremost among these extreme, and doomed, attempts to capture reality are the seemingly senseless, gratuitous acts of violence perpetrated by the "absurd criminal" who has become a negative culture hero of our time. Terrorizing our imaginations, if not our streets, he highlights an important social trend—our obsession with physical violence. But he also serves as a decoy; he deflects our attention from the more malignant forms of *psychological* violence which, often subtly disguised, pervade our society. The absurd criminal is, in the last analysis, a symptom, the physical embodiment of the less tangible atmosphere of manipulation and "mind-bending" which surrounds us. In trying to understand the enigmatic figure of the absurd criminal, we try to comprehend the abortive attempts of those marooned by unreality to give themselves a semblance of realness. But such understanding is incomplete if we lose sight of the backdrop of universal psychological violence, largely masked, against which these individual acts are silhouetted.

Let us start from a concrete example. In a recent book, the Swiss psychiatrist Medard Boss searchingly analyzes the case of an absurd criminal, F. F. This case is particularly fascinating because F. F.'s psychological profile resembles, in many respects, those of the Boston Strangler, of Charles Whitman, who picked off people like clay pigeons from his Texas University tower, and of Lee Harvey Oswald, the killer of John F. Kennedy.

F. F. was a Swiss office worker in his mid-twenties who almost committed a sex murder. He was walking one evening along the river Limmat with a girl he hardly knew when all of a sudden he was overcome by a wild urge to strangle her. He put his hands around her throat and began to press. Without question he would have murdered the girl if she had not somehow managed to free herself. Regaining his self-control, F. F. apologized to his dazed victim and said that he had not known what he was doing. Then he fled. He was so horrified by this sudden eruption of an irrepressible urge to kill that he sought psychiatric help.

During his psychiatric interviews it soon became evident that F. F. was a man dispossessed of his past. His self-image was as thin and hollow as a line drawing. In trying to tell his life story he only mangaged to come up with the most threadbare, schematic information; he might have been filling out a passport or employment application. One of the few events that stuck in his memory was a youthful romance of his early teens. This first amour had been destroyed, he felt, by a double betrayal: his mother had told his father about the boy's anxiously kept secret, and the father, in turn, had proceeded to "brutally stamp out" the tender idyll. Ever since, F. F. had been incapable of feeling much of anything for girls.

His family told the psychiatrist that from early childhood F. F. had kept coolly aloof from everybody. He did not join any family gatherings, even eating his meals by himself. At Christmas he refused to accept or give presents. It appeared that, from childhood on, F. F. was stuck in a psychological straitjacket. But he was not aware of this fact, nor of the dimness of his self-image.

F. F. was thoroughly estranged from the reality of himself. Hence it is really not surprising that he experienced many of his moods and deeds, including the murderous assault on the girl, as alien and divorced from the rest of his life. It simply did not occur to him to link the strangling attempt with an event that had taken place two weeks earlier. At that time he had been left by his mistress, a much older, unhappily married woman who had been the mainstay of his lonesome life. Her desertion hit him hard. He felt numbed by it, too numb to really experience his deep despair. Instead he developed excruciating headaches and vindictive fantasies about torturing and strangling his disloyal mistress. His urge to kill became increasingly intense and increasingly diffuse. In his waking life he soon "forgot" against whom his murderous rage was directed, but not in his dreams. Shortly before his brutal attack he dreamed that he was lost in an arid desert when he caught sight, in the far distance, of a burning farmhouse. He approached and saw his mistress standing, immobile, next to the burning house. He told her that he was going to kill her. Two nights later he almost strangled the substitute victim who chanced to cross his way.

In the course of therapy it turned out that long before the bizarre strangling attempt F. F. had dwelt in a world of (largely fantasied) violence. This was a very evident in his relationship with his mistress. He had felt initially distant and bored in his affair with her, as with all the other women whom he had tried out. Sexual intercourse with her was a mechanical "performance" meaning nothing. The shell of his aloofness was dented only when he began to bite and choke his mistress during intercourse. Then, for the first time in his adult life, genuine feeling for a woman stirred in him. The more brutal his acts became, the more his attachment grew.

The most important event of F. F.'s therapy was the gradual discovery that his sadistic rituals could not be taken at face value. On the face of it, he was angrily trying to torture and humiliate a woman he had rendered helpless. But a deeper impulse guided his sadistic sport. F. F. felt obscurely that he was trapped in the hard, rigid shell of a severe neurosis. Being thus imprisoned, a veritable Panzer Man, he could see others only as equally hidebound. And his sadistic games were precisely the psychic dynamite he needed to explode, for brief moments, the rigid casings of neurotic diffidence which kept him and his partner asunder. He wanted, as he put it, to "strip to the very core of the naked Adam" so that the hot current of communion could flow between him and the woman. Basically, he saw the whole sadistic rite as a mere overture, simply a transitional phase. Only by the black magic of brutality, he felt, could the two lovers' bodies be "melted in a single fire of love," culminating in a bottomless rapture of ecstatic union.

As long as his mistress was still with him, his sadistic acts enabled him intermittently to flee the prison of his stifling neurosis. But when his mistress left, his constriction became unendurable; only the violent explosion of a murder attempt could make him breathe for a while. In fact, he told the psychiatrist that this murderous eruption had not only shaken him but also given him a feeling of release.

Hence for F. F., and other sadists of his type, bizarre violence does not express only a wish to destroy and punish; it also constitutes an abortive attempt at appropriation— the miscarriage of an act of love. Having to break through the hard shell of a crippled personality, this loving intention is bound to take on grotesquely misshapen, explosive forms.

Dr. Boss's observations about the case of F. F. have been confirmed by this author and other therapists who have treated "absurd criminals." The theoretical interpretations of these cases may differ, but the basic data—the patients' early histories and personality structures—show striking parallels.

The case of F. F. and similar cases show that the absurd criminal looks absurd largely because his violence has been deflected from its authentic targets. The real objects of his hatred, those he aims to strike through the medium of his hapless, fortuitous victims, are usually close relatives or friends, wives, mistresses, sweethearts, or, most often, one or both parents. (From a psychological perspective, patricide and matricide are the most "rational" of crimes.) The absurd criminal has become absurd only because, having been victimized early in life, he had to disown his anger and rage, and had to forswear his knowledge of what his early oppressors had done to him, had to swallow the doctrine of their essential benevolence, and was thus reduced to lashing out—if at all—blindly, impulsively, and inanely against substitutes who had no real meaning in his life.

Modern depth psychology is a psychology of ambiguity, relying heavily on the notion of ambivalence which says that there are no "clean" motives. There are no acts of pure love, as there are no instances of unadulterated hatred. The idea of the unequivocal act, propelled by a single motive, is a pipe dream of the neurotic or the fanatic.

The notion of ambivalence helps us to unmask malignant forms of *psychological* violence which are much more far-reaching in their consequences than the quite circumscribed explosions of the criminal retailers of brute physical force. Erik Erikson's book *Ghandi's Truth* is instructive in this respect. Erikson shows that even the great Indian apostle of nonviolence displayed in his dealings with family and disciples a moral despotism, the coercive nature of which escaped only his own notice. His demanding absolutism was the more oppressive as it was supported by the authority of Gandhi's ascetic self-denial. But there was a price to be paid—often by others—for Gandhi's seeming immolation of selfhood.

Gandhi, in a flash of insight, once described himself as a "cruelly kind" husband. He imposed distasteful chores upon his wife, Kasturba, and expected her to do them *cheerfully*. Erikson suggests that it was probably this "cruel kindness" which estranged Gandhi's oldest son from him over the years. The son became a Moslem and eventually a derelict; within a year of the Mahatma's assassination he was found dead in "some locality."

Gandhi taught that violence is unjustifiable because "man is not capable of knowing the absolute truth and hence is not competent to punish," and yet he was not free from punishing vindictiveness. Erikson analyzes a curious incident related by Gandhi himself. The incident involved "mischievous" boys and "innocent" young girls bathing together at the suggestion of Gandhi, who wanted to test their self-restraint. When he was told that while bathing a young man had made fun of two of the girls, Gandhi got very upset. He concluded that the two girls, whose purity he felt to be compromised, must wear a visible mark on their person to "sterilize" a possible sinner's eye. He prevailed upon them, not without difficulty, to let him cut off their fine long hair. There was clearly violence in this, even if disguised as an act of "monastic ritualization" (as Erikson suggests).

Of course, Erikson's book is far from indicting Gandhi as a conscious hypocrite. The point is rather that he lacked the deep self-knowledge which would have made him aware of the ambiguity of human motives and of the nether side of coercion lurking behind the postures of nonviolence. But then, self-knowledge is usually beyond the grasp of those who aspire to sainthood.

If even Gandhi could not wholly transcend the laws of ambivalence, it is hardly surprising that, once our eyes are opened, we detect evidence of psychological violence all around us. Violence, we soon discover, is an integral part even of those institutions which are supposed to be models of nonviolence in our society, such as family, school, and mental hospital.

If one digs into the family backgrounds of neurotics addicted to brutality such as F.F., one is struck by the fact that, in some cases, the penchant for cruelty seems to have grown out of the soil of a normal, happy family. But a closer look usually shows us to be in the presence of one of those pseudo-normal families, so numerous in our culture, who cling to the ideology of compulsory happiness. The myth of the happy childhood dies hard, especially with those who were made to buy this myth by a process of brainwashing.

Even within the healthy family, raising a child involves all sorts of trespasses against his spirit. The child has to be made to follow the social decrees of the "correct," which preselect not only the answers he gets but eventually even the questions he asks. This tyranny of the "correct" constricts the child, making him alien to himself while predictable to others.

In a healthy family, the unavoidable savageries of the nursery are mitigated by genuine concern for the child's individuality. But with the pseudo-sane family, the child is ruthlessly exploited by his emotionally starved parents. The devices used to enslave the child are often quite subtle—and ominously effective. They are largely devices of humiliation and mystification by which the reality of the child's feelings is denied, distorted, or simply ignored. Many a child growing up in such a pseudo-democratic family is called "crazy" when he manages to pierce the deceptive facade of his parents' benevolence. Such a child has only two options: he may choose either to become a total outcast or to ignore the evidence of his senses.

Harold Searles, a Washington psychiatrist, has described such a child who was called "out of his mind" once too often. This young victim of schizoid parents came to totally distrust his own reactions and was reduced to using his pet dog as a sort of early warning system; from its tail waggings and similar signs he deduced whether a new acquaintance was well-intentioned or hostile and to be distrusted.

A patient of mine, a college dropout, had grown up in a family whose totalitarianism was carefully disguised. He came to see me because he was severely depressed. Also he was puzzled that he could not see any reason for his depression—no reason at all. He felt that he had had it easy. In the face of my questioning, he maintained steadfastly that his had been a particularly happy childhood and that he had been respected and loved by his family and his peers. He even once had started an autobiography with the statement: "Mine was the sunniest of childhoods, unmarred by adversity . . ." He was deeply convinced that his mother and stepfather had always been full of loving kindness, doing what was best for him. These declarations about his family's total bonhomie were unnervingly repetitious. They were practically the only information he volunteered during the first few months of therapy, which soon came to resemble a particularly painful version of *Waiting for Godot*.

He was one of those patients who do not dream. The first inkling that all was not for the best in his world came in connection with a concentration-camp dream which he produced after nine months of therapy, a dream that hit him with a shattering impact. It was shortly followed by a second dream in which he and his brothers were inflatable rubber toys which could be punctured and made to vanish by a mere pin prick. From then on he got hold of a trickle, and later a stream, of memories and feelings which gradually established beyond doubt that the presumed paradise of his childhood, in the reality of which he believed with such dogmatic fervor, had been in fact an ugly concentration camp.

This boy, whose case is not atypical, had been literally brainwashed by his doting family, who had no real place for him. He had been subjected to psychological terror which neither he nor his executioners recognized as such, but which reduced him to a sort of phantom, entirely out of touch with himself, unable to protest, dream, or feel. Among the main instruments of terror had been appeals to filial duty and to sweet reasonableness. His severe, life-endangering depression, misread by him and his "loved ones," was the only signal of distress he was able to produce.

The healthy family is a total environment for the young child; the pseudo-sane family degenerates into a totalitarian one. Its oppression is the harder to resist because it is usually masked by a pretense of limitless devotion.

The totalitarian atmosphere which envelops the life of the sick family also pervades those institutions which ought to be safe sanctuaries for the disabled victims of psychological brutality—the mental hospitals.

It is only too obvious that the equivocal figure of the psychiatric patient invites all sorts of psychological oppression. It is always easy to rationalize the use of violence against those who are allegedly bereft of reason. If we fail to see through these justifications, it is because they tend to adapt themselves to the ideological fashions of the day. It is true, as we are daily told by self-congratulatory medical authorities, that such crude forms of physical restraint as straitjackets and wet packs have pretty much vanished from our psychiatric wards. But this does not signify that violence itself has disappeared; it only means that more refined forms of coercion—whose coerciveness we tend to over-look—have come to the fore. If we can do away with physical straitjackets it may be because we have replaced them with less tangible, pharmaceutical ones.

The sociologist Erving Goffman has shown that even the best and best-intentioned mental hospital is, by virtue of its function and social structure, a total institution which of necessity dehumanizes its charges and subjects them to mortifying degradation ceremonies. Thus, to mention only one aspect, the admission procedure is usually most humiliating, especially for those who are pressured into committing themselves or are committed against their will. Admission is often preceded by what the patient-to-be can only interpret as a series of betrayals, beginning with his closest relative, who "turned him in." As soon as he has passed through the hospital doors, the neophyte patient is subjected to a series of interrogations which mercilessly probe his "weak spots." He then must undergo a stripping process which, even if it does not entail physical undressing and the donning of hospital garb, denudes him of his accustomed identity and defenses. He suddenly finds his status painfully reduced, his freedom of movement restricted, his privacy invaded and ignored; he is forced into close intimacy with people he may find uncongenial if not actually repulsive, and he discovers that he is under the diffuse authority of a whole echelon of people—psychiatric nurses, aides, doctors, administrators—who enforce a complex system of rules and may dish out stringent punishments. (Goffman notes that in the hospital he investigated, even the most regressed patients—those who were mute, incontinent, or halluci-nated—hardly ever dared to drop cigarette ashes on the linoleum floors; apparently, for their attendants, clean floors constituted the supreme value of ward life.)

The management of mental-hospital inmates involves one technique whose coercive nature is often ignored—the use of tranquilizers and other drugs. We do not usually think of Miltown or Librium as chemical straitjackets, but that is precisely how they may be viewed. This can become very obvious when a mental patient resists their use. Drugs that provide instant peace of mind are, in fact, primarily instruments of control. They do not cure, but they have the formidable virtue of prettying up the "raving maniac" or the incontinent catatonic. They also homogenize anger, anxiety, and depression into blandness, a feat greatly valued by our society.

But the traditional tranquilizers are modest in their aspirations by comparison with some newer drugs. A recent full-page advertisement in a journal of psychiatry features Haldol, billed as an antipsychotic drug. The large-lettered caption at the top of the ad asks: "How can you help him if he refuses medication?" The "he" of this caption turns out to be the "highly recalcitrant" psychotic patient who does not want to swallow prescribed drugs. Haldol has the curious distinction of being tasteless, colorless, and odorless. Hence, as the adman explains with laudable directness in colorless and odorless prose, it can be "added to any routine vehicle pleasing to the patient's taste, including fruit juice and even water." Now it is undoubtedly correct, as the copy writer implies farther on, that it is easier to subdue a resisting patient by slipping a detection-proof drug into his orange juice than by tying him up. It may also look more humane. But such low cunning, no matter how it is justified, degrades both its users and those against whom it is used. By masking violence, it tightens the web of mystification in which the patient is caught.

Another advertisement in the same journal, spread over several pages, promotes a drug called Aventyl HCl. It starts out with a large caption: "Do you have patients who try to hide frustration behind conformity?" The ad goes on to say: "You see many depressed patients who conceal their real emotional lives behind a veneer because it lets them hide from the finality of their depression. Before they come to you, few can recognize their despair. Even while seeking your help they may continue attempting to hide from you as well as themselves." Aventyl HCl has little sympathy for such pussy-footing. According to its promoters, it bestows miraculous, and somewhat contradictory, benefits; it is said to lift the patient's depression while forcing him to face the "finality" of it. It promises to dynamite psychic defenses and leave the person with no place to hide. One can only hope that this pharmaceutical prodigy fails to live up to its pretensions.

We have seen that the penchant for violence, whether open or subtly disguised, is rooted deep in the ambivalence of human nature. Ambivalence cannot be erased, but most people manage to come to terms with it. How do they differ from those who are prone to explode with violence?

To answer this question we must know that during normal personality growth ambivalence follows a fairly orderly process of evolution. According to the experts, first, right after birth, the infant lives through a preambivalent state of symbiotic fusion with the mother. This phase is short-lived. It is soon followed by a second, highly ambivalent stage during which intense love and violent hatred exist side by side, unconnected, in chaotic alternation. During this period the mother is split into two figures, the good fairy and the evil witch; later this process of splitting is extended to other persons. Throughout the long years of growing up, the crazy-quilt pattern of incoherent emotions is gradually sorted out; the fairy and the witch slowly become reconciled. If all goes well—if, in particular, the early expressions of anger are not curbed too brutally but are responded to as signals of distress—the child will eventually reach a point where he no longer experiences anger and hatred as devastating and ultimate. He will have learned to be angry without totally *being* his anger and without having to deny it. He will have accepted his ambivalence.

The violence-prone person, on the other hand, does not get that far. He becomes stuck during the early stages of chaotic ambivalence. Unable to slowly outgrow this painful and baffling chaos, he is made to suppress it harshly. He has to disown either his feelings of hatred or those of affection, thus becoming a model child or a professional villain; or, even more radically, he has to forswear *all* strong emotion, thus hardening himself into a cold schizoid statue.

Such a stunted person is always tempted to use violence, if only to make himself feel alive. In order to escape the sterile alternative of violence or numbness, he needs help. Opinions differ on how much we may expect from psychotherapy in this respect; the only statement we can make with confidence is that in certain cases it has helped people to outgrow the need for violence.

If even the sanctuaries of family and mental asylum are contaminated by the spirit of violence, it seems only natural to conclude—as our student rebels do—that our society at large is a total institution dealing in wholesale coercion which, much of the time, does not dare to avow its name. Their diagnosis may have some merit, but their prescription of redemption by militant counterviolence is as inadequate as a flabby doctrine of nonresistance which exhorts its faithful to go limp in the fact of actual or threatened violence.

If there is one lesson to be learned from cases like those of Boss's sadist F. F., it is precisely that the reverberating vicious circle of violence and counterviolence can be broken only by an attitude which is firm in containing violence but which is not provoked by provocation. Such an attitude we call therapeutic. This is not to say that such an attitude is the prerogative of psychotherapists, or that all or even most of them display it. It only means that psychotherapy at its nonambivalent best can show us a way out.

Thus psychiatric treatment enabled F. F. to abandon his poor religion of brutality. In order to get to this point he had to become daring enough to pass through a veritable orgy of verbal violence during which he battered his therapist with taunting and brutal insults, a period which lasted several months. And he could venture to do this only because his therapist was able, in the face of this onslaught, to sustain his attitude of benevolence without doing violence to his own feelings. The author knows of other ex-sadists who went through similar therapeutic experiences and who came to look at their whips and other tools of torture, which earlier had been the indispensable helpmates of their lust, with total incomprehension, as if they were prehistoric implements whose uses they had to puzzle out. Once these patients had outlived their infantile need for violence, they could no longer understand their earlier faith in the efficacy of sadistic rituals; it struck them as incredibly absurd that they had tried to whip others into loving them.

All this does not imply that psychotherapy is the only setting in which sadism and an addiction to violence can be outgrown. Such growth may also be promoted, most effectively, by the unlicensed quackery of life itself which, after all, is the most powerful of therapists. The point we wish to make is merely that the therapeutic situation, due to its unique protected structure, offers particularly favorable conditions for transcending the futile rituals of violence and counterviolence.

4

LSD

The Abortive Take-off*

As we have seen, the anesthetized neurotic, haunted by his sense of being unreal, may commit outlandish acts of violence in an attempt to blast a passageway to reality. Or he may try other, equally dubious expedients. He may try, by means of LSD or other hallucinogens, to vault straight into a cosmically and esthetically inflated surreality. He may seek to regain his sense of realness by losing himself in the oceanic mergings of symbiotic love. He may immerse himself in encounter groups with their potential for social amplification, hoping to have his reality defined by the intersecting realities of others. Or, settling for whatever version of reality is to be had from physical thrills, he may

* This chapter was written in collaboration with Charles C. McArthur.

77

get astride a souped-up motorcycle, driving it out into the control of centrifugal force, "on the high side," where the merciless power of momentum plays God with his fate.

But a reality which has become stale and tarnished cannot be restored by the contriving of cheap kinetic thrills; it cannot be disposed of by drug-induced "transcendence"; nor can fragments of keyed-up sensations, no matter how artfully devised, be made to coalesce into the relative coherence of a real world. By impaling himself upon a reality contorted into lacerating jaggedness, the prisoner of the unreal may find a short reprieve from his numbness. But in the end, reality proves intractable; it cannot be coerced into renewing itself.

To what lengths the quest for latent realities may go is illustrated by the recent revival of the "witch's chair," an invention of the Middle Ages. This device, reactivated by a contemporary psychologist, consists of a kind of flying saucer with a cagelike superstructure, suspended by a spring from a cable at the top, so that the slightest movement of its passenger will cause sway. A blindfolded rider in the chair soon loses orientation, as the free-floating device responds in feedback to his every intended or unintended motion. The effect is not unlike sensory deprivation (another current fashion—research fads reflect the Zeitgeist) and the "witch" is soon riding through autistic space, providing his or her own Walpurgisnacht.

The revival of the witch's chair is, of course, an attempt to provide a drugless, low-risk version of the mescaline, peyote, and LSD trips which Aldous Huxley and his lesser acolytes, the Learys and Alperts, sold with the aid of glossy-picture tracts as a new form of mass tourism to our travel-hungry age. The idea of using vision-inducing drugs to unveil latent realities was hardly new, but the messianic hucksterism propagating a cheap mass exodus to "inner space" probably was. At any rate, for so many of our contemporaries to prove susceptible to such a gospel, the reality they were inhabiting must have felt to them very arid and insipid indeed.

It is in fact much more a hunger for latent, and nourishing, realities than a hedonistic quest for a blissful nirvana which motivates a great many drug users of our days. Their goals are high-minded, however dubious their means. They have been called "experience seekers" by Zinberg and others, in opposition to the oblivion seekers who were predominant in earlier periods of American history. It has been largely forgotten by now how widespread the use of opium was before 1914. In the harsh Bureau of Narcotics era that followed, marijuana managed to survive, perpetuated at first by the rural poor in the South and Southwest, then spreading north, with migrations, till it became widely known in urban slums during the Great Depression. Its use was for solace, not for thrills; but solace is, as Coles remarks, "no small thing for fearful men and women." Heroin seems to have existed (since the Harrison Act) mostly in the cities, used also among the poor, and also for the solace of oblivion. It is still mostly used so today. When one gets to know heroin addicts by means of psychological tests, one is awestruck by their inner emptiness; their endopsychic landscape resembles a lunar wasteland. It is the agonizing pain of this emptiness, as much as the squalor of their milieu, which they must obliterate by their fix.

The experience seekers, feeding on lysergic acid, mescaline, peyote, psilocybin, and other hallucinogens, are also driven by psychic hunger, by a more or less clear sense of inner emptiness. But their emptiness is not so extreme as to seem beyond redemption. Their hunger, their pain, is energizing rather than merely debilitating. They use drugs, in Zinberg's words, "not to get away from life but to embrace it . . . [for] a feeling that a level of genuine experience which is closed to them by their culture is opened for them by the drug." If *they* swallow lysergic acid or mescaline, it is because they want to embark upon "reality trips." But the realities which the drugs hustle up for them remain, in the end, disappointingly ephemeral. They tend to evaporate without leaving much of a residue.

This is not to say that something "real" does not happen to the experience seeker while he is tripping. On the contrary, innumerable travelogues of drug users leave little doubt that experiences of the greatest import, ranging from ecstatic bliss to absolute horror, are vouchsafed to them in that altered state. These experiences often carry with them an overwhelming sense of realness, and to utterly deny them this attribute means to use the word "real" in the overly narrow and dogmatic way which has been questioned throughout this book. If the solace of oblivion is no small thing for the fearful, it is also no small thing for people trapped in a gray dismal existence to experience at first hand, with an overpowering evidential quality, the emergence of usually veiled worlds of seemingly inexhaustible richness which wait only for the magic touch of release to come to the fore. The exaltation may be fleeting, the price of admission high, but one can hardly blame the prisoners of dreariness if they do a bit of gate-crashing to partake, for brief moments, of the feasts of life where the "imaginary" passionately embraces the "real," waxing more powerful than tangible reality itself.

Let us listen, for a moment, to the testimony of such a temporary escapee from constriction. In his book *The Beyond Within* Sidney Cohen tells the story of a college student whom he is at pains to describe as "an ordinary guy" and who in the wake of his first LSD trip wrote a letter to his girl describing his experience. Part of the letter reads:

. . . The last of the long-desired "visual effects" are now wearing off, the last of the numbness, the last of the gnawing pain in my stomach. But yet something remains behind; it has left something—I guess you might say a footprint, in the eternity which has come into existence since it first began to wreak its little havoc of hell and heaven, of orgasm and pain, and fear and hope, and beauty and filth. Ruth, I can't explain what it was like. I remember saying, "It's too much for me, it's too much." Was I afraid! I felt like a little boy, a naked, bare-faced little boy. And I pleaded, "Please stop, I don't want to see me." But it came anyway; and it overwhelmed me like the ocean washing over a little boy's sand castle despite the little dikes and moats. . . .

. . . I sat in the restaurant just enjoying living. Everything seemed so clear and beautiful. It was like looking at the world for the very, very first time and thinking to yourself, how beautiful, how sensuous! . . . I watched the ice water, the water on the counter top, the reflection of the ceiling in the water . . . I watched the cheese melt on top of my hamburger. Have you ever watched the foam on a glass of beer? What a world of delight can exist in such a common thing. . . .

I suddenly realized what I had meant by saying it's too much. I had the wrong slant on it. The world looked to me like it must to a little child, all big and beautiful. And I was experiencing it without the imposed controls that we have to slap on in order to become adults. I think I was afraid that my hold on the difference between the child's and the adult's world wasn't too firm—and all those sights were just too overwhelming. As I was out walking I was, literally, experiencing the world as a child would, and I loved it and didn't give a damn about what anybody thought. I was almost drunk with rapture and I felt like bursting. . . .

We have purposely chosen the letter of this rather naïve student who was not gifted with the visionary power or the eloquence of a Baudelaire or Ginsberg, but in whom LSD tapped a vein of genuine lyricism. Also his letter contains several elements fairly typical of psychedelic visions. His emphasis on seeing the world with the fresh eyes of the child reminds one of Huxley's remark that under mescaline his universe became as startlingly new and supernaturally brilliant as it must have appeared to Adam on the morning of his creation. And our student's discovery of the esthetic and metaphysical depths of the foam on a glass of beer has its counterpart in Huxley's seeing "Eternity in a flower, Infinity in four chair legs and the Absolute in the folds of a pair of flannel trousers!" But apparently the most important aspect of the psychedelic experience for our letter writer, and many others, was the mere fact of its giving a direct glimpse of another, vibrantly alive reality which beggared, and revealed the deadness of, their shadowy everyday world.

But it is this everyday reality to which the escaped prisoner must return in the end. And if it is true—as our letter writer and other initiates claim—that the hallucinogenic vision leaves behind a footprint of Eternity, the question poses itself: how durable is this imprint, how does it bear upon, and how much does it transform, the returnee's way of dealing with the exigencies of everyday life? Realities that are not actively appropriated and embodied in our daily existence do fade and become "unreal." It is our impression that of the various forms of visions we have examined so far—dreams, spontaneous hallucinations, drug-induced visions—the latter are most difficult to assimilate, and most vulnerable to the fate of sterile evaporation.

Perhaps this sterility is the price to be paid for gate-crashing. The experiences with LSD-therapy bear on this point. High hopes were pinned initially on the therapeutic virtues of this drug which seemed to short-circuit the laborious process of reducing neurotic defenses. The proponents of LSD-therapy, suffering from a curious form of collective amnesia, seemed to have forgotten the earlier lessons learned from work with pentothal, amytal, hypnosis, etc. All these agents which seemed to promise therapeutic short cuts were disappointing in the end. They were effective at tearing down or circumventing psychic defenses, as is LSD. They were, in fact, too effective; they would churn up more repressed material than the ego could handle. The same is true for LSD and other hallucinogens. Personality growth simply cannot be force-fed by short-circuiting the ego.

If tranquilizing drugs such as Librium or Valium are said to be antitherapeutic in that they perform a sort of chemical lobotomy, much the same can be said of hallucinogens. They also are mutilating agents. By rendering large tracts of the ego inoperative, they make it unlikely that the surfacing images can be fixed and digested. Hallucinogens typically distort the user's perception of time. They may put him on a perpetually moving, dizzying merry-go-round where sights and feelings alternate too quickly to crystalize into durable impressions. They may also slow down time till—as reported by Gautier—it takes "at least ten years" to get from the center of a drawing room to its door, but this time whose motion has been reduced or suspended is, as a rule, curiously vacant. In either case, there is little food for the ego.

There is still another, often ignored, aspect which renders the hallucinogens antitherapeutic. These drugs which dynamite psychic defenses are pregnant with violence—a violence directed mainly against the user's self. At the most tangible level, there are undesirable physiological effects: dryness of the throat, vascular constriction, dizziness, nausea, headaches, vomiting. These symptoms are played down by labeling them as mere "side effects." But can physical toxicity be exorcised by verbal magic? Hardly. One wonders about the jauntiness with which people apt to worry about the poisoning of their physical environment ingest drugs whose known toxic effects are not trivial and whose less-known long-range effects are suspected, at least by some investigators, of being much more ominous. The point is not to dramatize the risks inherent in the use of these drugs, but rather to inquire into the motives of users who lightly dismiss such risks. It seems plausible that many who are drawn to hallucinogens are so precisely because they cater both to consciously held motives (search for a new reality or a new high) and to darker, more submerged (masochistic) ones. A patient who maintained that he took

LSD for the sole purpose of making himself feel good later came to realize that he was at the same time, without knowing it, "paying bills to his unconscious." His conscious euphoria was bought at the price of unconscious self-destruction. For some, this covert self-punishment may even be the most enticing feature of the drug ritual.

On occasion, the malignant harshness implicit in drug use becomes pretty obvious. Thus a singularly bad drug synthetized by the young alchemists of the California beaches was sardonically christened "LBJ," but in spite of its objectionable features, acknowledged on the label, the drug continued to be made and used by young people unaware of the full extent of their latent masochism. They seemed actually to welcome the violence of the side effects while at the same time denying it by their casual diction.

It is not only the camouflaged harshness of hallucinogens which is too often ignored. Hardly ever mentioned is another feature of the drug experience which in clinical jargon would be called "displacement," which occurs when, in the presence of an anxiety-fraught situation, a person's attention is deflected from the really crucial factors to lesser ones. A case in point is that of the phobic person who can cross a street only when he is in the company of a friend; otherwise he gets paralyzed or suffers a severe anxiety attack. His phobia leads him to focus his whole attention on the anxiety connected with crossing the street; the need for the presence of another person is for him, so to speak, only a side effect of this disabling anxiety. But in actuality it is his need for the closeness of another person, and his anguish at being alone, which is psychologically primary. This anguish, being unbearable for the phobic neurotic, gets displaced onto the phobic impediment. Then the desperate need for another person can be brought into play surreptitiously, without having to be fully acknowledged.

Now the use of hallucinogens may involve quite similar legerdemain, with the drug becoming a sort of magic eye-catcher. Thus the rituals of tripping usually require the presence of others. Ordinarily one does not trip alone, but needs at least one other person who officially functions as guide or as a sort of safety net. This other person is usually thought of as an extra, one of the paraphernalia of the drug experience. But what if, as in the case of the phobic, his presence were much more crucial than is commonly acknowledged? What if it were the surreptitious satisfaction of libidinal needs, as much as the physical effects of the drug itself, which enable the tripper to gain enough elan to take off? What, in other words, if a major function of the drug were to act as an attention-diverting placebo?

That such possibilities ought not to be ignored is underlined by the author's observation that plain, drugless psychotherapy can produce, in quite a few patients, all the vaunted effects—including the more extravagant perceptual, esthetic, comological, and psychological "highs"—usually attributed to the specific action of hallucinogens. And for these drugless, gimmickless trippers it is most likely that the libidinal bond to the therapist functions as their magic carpet.

In general, drug users tend to overestimate the stimulus value of hallucinogens. Drugs do not "cause," in any meaningful sense of the term, the so-called hallucinogenic experience, as the stylus of our stereo does not "cause" the music filling our room. To the extent that hallucinogens are effective, they act as catalysts releasing latent images stored in the mind. Far from obliterating individual differences, they often highlight them. Take, for instance, the differences in the reports on their hashish visions by the nineteenth-century French authors Gautier and Baudelaire, who are among the more noted literary observers of drug-induced states. As Grinspoon points out, Gautier's chief orientation was esthetic and artistic, and his drug experiences correspondingly involved worlds of fantastic colors and shapes, a heightened visual sense; whereas Baudelaire, much more analytical and given to philosophic and moral speculations, experienced overwhelming abstractions dealing with God and the devil. Or take the case of a patient in his mid-thirties who spent most of his life in self-contained isolation but whose long-denied needs for human warmth began slowly to emerge in the decompression chamber of therapy. One evening, under mescaline, he suddenly asked a male friend to hold his hand, explaining that he felt a desperate need for a lifeline. This action was atypical for this previously aloof person; it was premature in terms of where he was at in his conscious life. Obviously the drug had not created the impulse for closeness, it had simply catalyzed its upsurge.

This being-out-of-phase with the person's conscious development is another factor responsible for the relative sterility of many drug experiences. Also the use of hallucinogens often results in cosmological projections or abstract speculations which lead the person away from confronting his buried psychological reality. For example, a neurotic patient under the influence of LSD drew a point in the middle of a circle. During his LSD state, he saw this as a very apt image of his psychological situation: he himself was the shriveled-up point in the middle, surrounded on all sides and circumscribed, not able to reach the confining walls or to go beyond. In a later therapy hour he reported this experience. He was invited by his therapist to condense these rather abstract, general notions into more concrete images. Instantly it occurred to the patient that what he had drawn was a woman's breast, and this recognition set off an amazing cascade of memory images. An image of his mother's breast emerged, memories of being told that she fell ill briefly after giving birth; apparently she was given contradictory advice about breastfeeding by two doctors, and chose to follow the doctor who told her to stop nursing. Then images of his wife's breasts flashed into his mind; at first she seemed very beautiful, but then he caught a glimpse of her face clouded by pain. Immediately the breasts change to lifeless, flopping appendages, mere lumps of flesh. He saw himself shuttling back and forth between his wife's breasts and his mother's breasts, then became an infant sucking at the breast of a former mistress of his. Deeply lacerating, anguished feelings of never having been really pacified began to emerge.

This patient had been very intent all along upon breaking through the confining walls of neuroticism to find his hidden self. This was his reason for entering therapy and for earlier experiments with drugs. He took LSD in the spirit of the reality seeker. But his drug-elicited images did not connect, and when he began to experience "monster vibrations" during a bad trip, he forswore lysergic acid. This was rather ironical, for it is precisely the scary horror show of the bad trip which is most likely to bring the experience seeker face to face with his hidden self. He thus very often abandons, as our patient did, his quest at the very point where it might begin to yield what he is looking for—a fragment of pure, unadulterated reality.

We conclude that, by and large, hallucinogens fall short of providing easy short cuts to the hidden self; they are more likely to lead to dead ends. The tawdry harshness of the means employed, the greedy reaching for instant revelations are ultimately self-defeating.

Much the same is true for the proliferating attempts to find one's self in encounter groups. The latent realities elicited by encounter techniques prove, in the end, as disappointing as those conjured up by chemicals.

It is our impression that many, if not most, encounter groups are imbued with a spirit of grossness and contempt for their participants' modesty which mocks their claims to enhance "sensitivity." Bludgeoning desensitization and coarse disregard for the individual's vulnerability seem too often to prevail. The person's tender spots may be exposed and probed without mercy. One example of many cited in a recently published book: a woman who is self-conscious about her body displays her nude self to the group in an imaginatively gross way while the group leader lectures her on how bad it is for her to be so negative about her sex organs. His announced purpose is to overcome her self-consciousness. One wonders about the meaning, and also the practical results, of such curious procedures. One is hardly reassured by learning that the victims of these pseudo-therapeutic ministrations often declare afterward that the forcible subversion of their modesty has done them a world of good. It is an odd commentary on our times that the American Psychological Association has of late been reviewing the terms of its group malpractice insurance to cope with lawsuits arising from physical injuries suffered by members of encounter groups. The encounters in such

89

groups must be pretty vigorous if safeguards against bodily injury are needed which one had associated, so far, mostly with automobile insurance. Unfortunately, the psychic injuries incurred in such robust group activities are less actionable.

But even groups relatively free from excessive harshness are rarely conducive to enticing the person's latent reality out of hiding. Few, if any, groups can provide the sort of quiet, safe, intrusion-proof echo chamber which is most apt to make a person hear the faint, ignored whisperings of his hidden self. Random collections of disparate, often anonymous, men and women, encounter groups can hardly provide the warm, dependable, unshakable support which alone enables man to dare confront his denied, or ignored, reality. Regression, the return to one's myth-shrouded personal beginnings, is the central venture promoted, more or less wittingly, by most encounter groups (and by most other therapeutic endeavors). But to invite a person to regress without giving him the unquestioning acceptance which alone can make such returns upon oneself fruitful is foolish or criminally irresponsible; it will insure either the miscarriage of the attempt to regress—the more likely outcome—or, more rarely, the anguish of psychotic disarray without the recompense of personal growth.

Lest we be misunderstood: there is no implication here that the person can do for himself, by himself, what drugs and encounter groups fail to do for him. To fully realize his hidden self—that is, to fully realize the depth and singularity of his aloneness—man needs the affirmative presence of a parentlike other who finds part of his own fulfillment in promoting growth. This mysterious, searing aloneness in the presence of the helping other, who both asserts and denies separateness, is the fruitful paradox which is at the core of psychotherapy as a process of raising the latent reality unrealized within us.

5

THERAPY

The Self Reclaimed

To be the midwife of the patient's denied reality, the conjurer, spokesman, and gentle exorcist of his ghosts: this is the definition of the therapist's task implicit in the preceding chapters. In the present, final chapter, this task will be made more explicit. It requires the therapist to take, unswervingly, the side of the patient's "unreality"—of his disowned fantasies, visions, intuitions, dreams. By supporting the shadowy apparitions trapped between being and nonbeing, by helping the patient to sustain their full impact, the therapist makes them a part of the person's lived reality, and, in doing so, enriches it.

The patient's dilemma is that his surfacing reality is flickering and intermittent. It may manage to totally eclipse, for a while, the old established reality, but its preponderance will be short-lived. Very soon the original belief in the veracity of the new vision will turn into denial and doubt. Then doubt itself will become doubtful. The patient will sway back and forth, indecisively and painfully, between embracing his new reality and repudiating it. Like Allen Ginsberg, he will wonder whether his brain is cracked or whether he has come upon a deeper truth than had been vouchsafed him up to then. At this point of unstable equilibrium, the therapist's intervention will be decisive. By simply stating, in a simple way, his faith in the truth of the emerging reality, he will make it more viable for the patient.

Sometimes the doubt which the patient has to overcome is felt by him as a tangible physical force.

A patient in his late twenties, whose story we will refer to again later, stumbled in therapy upon a forgotten childhood drama which, he was sure, had set the whole course of his life. In the incident in question, he had discovered his mother and uncle in bed in his grandparents' guest room. When it first resurfaced, the traumatic scene did so very vividly, with a great wealth of detail. But very soon the magic transparencies became cloudy, and doubt set in. The patient did not deny that the whole scene *felt* very real to him, but he became painfully aware of the lack of corroborating evidence. Actually, doubt whispered to him, the scene clashed with everything he *knew* about his mother, and almost certainly had been concocted by his therapeutically overheated mind.

The patient's struggle to establish the mendacity of the scandalous memory took on epic proportions. At one point, he saw himself trying to run down a corridor to the door of the fatal guest room where his mother's betrayal had taken place, but found himself held back by a fierce wind which was sweeping through the apartment and rooting him to the spot. Only by the subterfuge of shrinking himself to the size of a tiny boy and running madly, like a streak, *under* the wind, did he finally manage to get moving. But now his élan was such that he overshot the guest room and crashed through the retaining wall at the end of the corridor, hurtling off into space.

In the next therapy hour, he was able to reposition himself in the forbidden room and to resurrect its furniture, but the place on the bed where his mother and her lover should be was blanked out. It seemed first to be covered by a gauzy veil, then completely "matted out" by a process familiar to photographers, leaving nothing but a black hole. But it was a sonorous hole emitting animal-like bleats and snarls. The patient commented on how distinctly and clearly he could see the flower pattern of the wallpaper, and the rest of the room. He could almost hear a mocking voice telling him: "The background you may see, in as much detail as you want, because it does not prove anything."

While he was still struggling to push aside the blackness which prevented him from seeing, he told a series of dreams he had dreamed the previous night (which was the first night after his rediscovery of the traumatic scene). These dreams were quite disparate in content, loosely strung together by one thread: they kept reiterating, in various forms, that the patient was not trustworthy, and, in doing so, they seemed bent on discrediting him as a witness. It was the patient who first picked up this theme and drew the logical conclusion: if he could be made to believe, by means of dreams or otherwise, that he was but a poor meretricious witness, then the traumatic scene was bound to lose its credibility and could be relegated to the realm of imagination.

This inventive patient used various other devices to de-realize what he had seen. But the therapist's support solidified the emerging reality. All the therapist needed to do was to question the voices that kept calling the patient names, to encourage him to focus his images, and to convey his faith in the realness of the vistas unfolding in the patient's mind. His therapist's trust enabled the patient, who was a past master at equivocation, to finally state with a new-found boldness that the only reality that mattered was the reality in his head—his own reality.

The author has found it useful, in this business of therapeutic midwifery, to deal with common-sense reality in a high-handed manner. Far from recognizing its claim to be "objectively" given," I treat it as if it were infinitely plastic, subject to the sovereign whims of the individual. More radical than the Freudians, I refuse to make concessions to their prim "reality principle." By dealing with the patient as if he were a powerful magician who shapes the seemingly most accidental, uncontrollable events of his life, I make him push against the prison walls of his too narrowly construed reality. To take an extreme example: if a patient is late for a session because his brand-new car, which he had no reason to distrust, broke down on the way to my office, I look at his lateness as if it was willed by him. I am tentative rather than dogmatic about this, and will not crowd him very hard. I will not worry about the mechanisms by which his postulated wish to be late transmitted itself to his car. But time after time I find my "naïve" assumption—that reality is much more pliable to our unconscious wishes than we commonly assume—rewarded by the surfacing of rich clinical material. (Another way of looking at the same event is that I deal with the incapacitated car as if it were a living organism, a horse; it is most unusual for a horse, whether young or old, to break down without warning, without the prior appearance of some premonitory signs, possibly quite faint.) I have found it equally fruitful to think of my patients' physical diseases, even those diagnosed as "purely organic," as if they were unconsciously willed. Of course, there is nothing very new about this sort of radical psychologism. Its main justification, in the present context, is that it works. It helps to conjure up ghosts which otherwise would have remained quite invisible.

To put it differently: as therapist I look at external reality with the eyes of a surrealist painter who penetrates stereotyped surface appearances and dissolves their realistic contours (which seem "naturally given" to most of us, but are the result of a complex process of overlearning) in order to see the visual field swayed and constellated by the underlying currents of fantasy and emotion which determine, in the last analysis, our manner of seeing and the appearance which the objects of our world present to us.

This therapeutic surreality which temporarily de-realizes our everyday world is, at bottom, a reality of *feeling*. That is, its core is irrational. But it is only the wholehearted affirmation of this irrational core by the individual which allows a true rationality to emerge. This statement about the primacy of feeling does not aim to be metaphysical; it does not claim to pronounce itself on the ultimate nature of reality. It merely states, as directly as possible, that for the neurotic and psychotic the denied reality is, in the last analysis, a reality of disowned emotion, which means a

reality that is *concrete* and *specific*. This definition out-
lines the task of the therapist, if not necessarily the method
by which to accomplish this task.

I like to think of the kind of therapy I am doing as "realness therapy." (I would call it "reality therapy" if somebody else who is actually doing unreality therapy had not
pre-empted this label.) We need not worry too much
whether it is new or original or how much it differs from what
others do. I feel in fact that this widespread concern about
therapeutic patents is undesirable; it gets us sidetracked
into sterile polemics, rigidifies our posture, and by inducing
us to exaggerate marginal differences, easily deflects us from
the path which we would have otherwise followed and
which is properly our own. Besides, it is unlikely that anybody in this field is going to invent totally new techniques.
The claim to have done so is usually only a measure of a
man's ignorance of the history of his discipline. Almost
everything that is advertised as new has been tried by someone else before. Whatever originality there is has not to do
with new technical gimmicks but only with a new and
personal perspective, a quasi-artistic resynthesis which gives
new meaning to old tools. Such a new synthesis which
makes things fall into place in a different way may seem of
lesser import, to the nonperceptive, than the fabrication of
a supposedly new technique, but its consequences are far
more extensive. At any rate, authors who worry too much
about the newness of what they say are unlikely to be
original. It seems best to put down our views as simply and
succinctly as possible, and let history and gossips worry
about their novelty.

Given the basic premises that neurotic miseries arise from
unreality, that therapy is the quest for the real self, and

that the fundamental reality of this self is a reality of feeling, we shall want to ask: what are the features of the therapeutic setup, and of the therapist himself, which are most favorable to the unfolding of the unrealized self?

Let us look first at the therapeutic situation. One of its key features is that, in subtle ways and with society's blessings, it is surrounded with safeguards which make it self-perpetuating. This may sound like a bad joke or a bit of cynicism, but it is neither. In order for the patient to dare to expose the raw, undeveloped parts of his self, he needs to be secure from abrupt withdrawal by his therapeutic partner. He must be confident that the therapeutic bond is durable enough to survive the vagaries of shifting moods.

The ritual aspects of therapy (e.g., regular schedule, the preset length of each session) and its basic social definition (a professional relationship aimed at achieving long-term goals) are such as to minimize the risks of premature disruption. A major stabilizing factor is the *fee* which the patient pays the therapist. This fee compensates, to some extent, for the basic asymmetry of the patient-therapist relation. It helps to persuade the therapist to do something for a relative stranger which most of us can do naturally (and then not always easily) only for our own children: namely, to deny for a prolonged period, within the setting of a quite intense relationship, the expression of our own vital needs, to push them aside and ignore them for the sake of the self-discovery of another person. The therapist can do this not because he is endowed with superhuman, self-denying generosity, but because the situation in which he finds himself engaged with the patient is, in spite of its intensity, somewhat artificial. (It is one of the many apparent paradoxes of therapy that the artificiality of the therapeutic situation is one of the preconditions for the reality of the patient to emerge.)

The therapeutic situation is not quite "for" real for the therapist in the sense that he does not expect from it the satisfaction of his more basic needs, but this does not prevent it from being extremely real for the patient. It is precisely this quasi-unreality of his bond to the patient which allows the therapist to remain in a situation that makes so many demands upon him and rewards him mostly in counterfeit coin: money. (The ritualized, one-sided exchange of money is itself a sign of de-realization.) Thus the artificiality of the therapeutic setup protects the neurotic against the recurring catastrophe of his everyday life—that is, being deserted by those he needs. His unrealness drives them away, and he fears, not without reason, that if he dares to be more genuine and displays his real (neurotically deformed) feelings he will now produce the same end result. This is the tragic dilemma in which he finds himself caught.

It is ironic that many neurotics protest loudly against this artificiality of the therapeutic setup. They feel somehow humiliated by it—mainly because it confronts them with their helplessness and dependency—and they struggle mightily to change the situation and to transform the therapist into a friend. What they do not realize is that if they were to succeed, it would spell the failure of the therapeutic enterprise. For friendship is based on a better balance of mutual give-and-take than the neurotically needy person is able to offer. The life history of the neurotic is usually a convincing, endlessly repeated demonstration that, for him, the dream of self-realization through friendship is a delusion (because what he needs is not a friend but a parent or the closest possible facsimile thereof); as in so many other respects, he is unable to assimilate, because of his neurotic blind spots, this important lesson of his life history.

Of course, whether the person in therapy can reach his goal and gets hold of his own reality depends, in the end, on the realness of the therapist. The demands on him are enormous. In order to do his job of midwifery well, the therapist ought to be a paragon of contradictory virtues. He ought to be sensitive but robust, kind but not easily seduced, warm without being seductive, a seer of ghosts who has his feet firmly on the ground, flexible as Proteus yet endowed with integrity. He ought to have the improvising touch and the radar antennae of the artist who discovers and makes visible what is invisibly present rather than indulging in arbitrary invention. He simply cannot go by the book and the rules of orthodoxy, but must improvise his way over an ever-changing, only partly mapped terrain full of pitfalls that make continuous demands on his ingenuity.

The therapist is confronted, much of the time, with an infinity of choices. He may hide from himself the fact that there are no prearranged highways to reality by clinging to Freudian or other orthodoxies. He may oversimplify reality by attempting to make it conform to behavioristic notions, or he may overcomplicate it by trying to catch it in a net of baroquely convoluted theories. But if his powers of imagination are not hopelessly crippled, he will find himself, again and again, at crossroads of great complexity where no theory can point out to him *the* correct road, where the notion of *the* correct road itself may be absurd, and where he must depend, in the end, on his intuition to decide which path may be the shortest one to his chosen destination, or which one is most likely to be negotiated by a particular patient. It is one of the saving graces of therapy that there are few, if any, definite dead ends. If the therapist is not too rigid he can always retrace his steps and strike out in a new direction, thus transforming a potential dead end into a mere detour.

As we have already seen, one of the temptations to which the therapist is exposed is the temptation to manipulate or coerce his patient, to use more or less covert violence. Unfortunately, this temptation is not always resisted, nor even recognized as such. The violent therapist is an inevitable and frequent by-product of our violence-prone society.

In fact, a growing number of therapists use very robust methods, the violence of which seems often to be hidden only from its perpetrators and, sometimes, their victims. It is argued that these techniques which assault and humiliate the patient do work. But, as W. H. Auden has pointed out, so does torture. Such brutal techniques are much used by schools which enjoy a vogue of late—Gestaltists, Primal Therapists, Reichians, and various encounter cults. Sometimes the assault is mounted directly against the victim's flesh. His body is undressed, palpitated, massaged. It looks as if the therapist were literally trying to tear the incubus neurosis out of the sufferer's gut. Some descriptions of the forceful massage techniques used by Reichians to break down the "muscle armor" of neurotics remind one of the medieval treatment of heretics by means of the wheel and the rack. Other therapists are physically less vigorous but rely on the curative effects of *psychological* bullying. Thus the late Fritz Perls, a leader of the Gestalt school, would put his victims, in front of an audience, on a chair designated as "hot seat," and, if the mood struck him (as it did quite frequently), pound them with merciless questions and sarcasms. The primal therapist Janov calls his patients "fag," "loser," "midwestern hick," and other names, and he may lock the door in their face when they leave his office to urinate, or threaten to get rid of them for good if they are "neurotically late."

Equally questionable are the "touch" techniques promoted by various encounter cults. These techniques, based on the fiction of instant, group-produced intimacy, take an overly simplistic view of the human body and its meaning. If we grant that a person's body is at least as delicate and easily untuned as a musical instrument, we might wonder what we would expect from, say, a violin exposed to fingering and thumping by everyone who came along. To make the neurotic bare his body to the look and touch of relative strangers will cause him to "steel" himself against such contact and, in spite of his verbal testimony to the opposite, will drive his buried feelings farther underground. The gap between his real self and his body will be widened. He will thus pay the penalty for ignoring the basic fact that the truth of feeling cannot be coerced.

One wonders about the vogue of such drastic procedures. Of course, it is a key fantasy of the walled-in neurotic who is so common these days that his stubborn defenses can be reduced only by violent means. Every day, neurotic patients who despair of getting rid of their unreality plead with their therapists to "break them." But we must not be too quick to oblige. Neurotics are notoriously prone to confuse poison with medicine, or to ask for poison because they do not believe that a true medicine exists. What the neurotic actually may express when he asks the therapist to break him is his conviction that this is the best deal he can get: if he satisfies the therapist's yen for power, the latter may be interested enough to get involved with him. The patient behaves in this respect like a masochist who clings to his sadistic lover because he cannot really believe that a better option exists, that someone might actually love him without wanting to hurt him. Similarly, the neurotic's early experience has not prepared him to give credence to the notion of a relatively selfless parental figure whose will to help does not disguise a wish to exploit. The idea of a gentle, dependable, unpossessive, and unvengeful parental helper who disdains coercion is beyond his ken. Hence if a neurotic implores us to do him violence for "his own good," let us try to widen his horizon rather than to narrow our own.

What is the goal of psychotherapy? Is it to unleash explosive affects at any price? If so, there is much to be said for the frontal assault methods à la Janov, Perls, Reich, and others. It is true that these methods can trigger off intense feelings in heavily defended neurotics. But what their proponents overlook is over half a century of dubious long-range results of such strong-arm techniques. After all, Freud started out with cathartic purging of repressed emotions—a method "reinvented" several times since, most recently by Janov—only to discover that a violently induced hemorrhage of the patient's feelings, even though offering temporary relief, is of about as much lasting curative effect as the thorough bleedings and purges to which Molière's physicians would subject their charges. In both cases, the patients would be less tense, because exhausted, but hardly much healthier.

If to cure a neurosis were as simple as to dynamite, by any available means, the patient's defenses, then we would expect that psychotic experience as such would be conducive to superhealth. After all, psychosis is the great natural leveler of defenses and emancipator of stifled affects. But psychosis, in and by itself, is hardly growth-promoting; it needs much laborious effort by the ego to integrate the denied contents, released by the psychotic breakdown of defenses, into the conscious personality, and thus make madness a road to, rather than away from, the individual's reality. There is a world of difference between the unloosing of constipated feelings and the bringing forth of a new reality which fits our deepest vision without making us unfit for everyday tasks. This new reality, to be sure, will encompass the spontaneous truth of our feelings, but also must enter the laborious synthesis of our intellect which alone gives form and duration to this truth.

Also, there is the *moral* point to be considered which, in the field of psychotherapy, is apt to be a very practical point. To assault a human being grossly or subtly, no matter how noble the assailant's intentions, means to be contemptuous of whatever reality the person owns at that point. The therapist may think that this reality is fake and neurotic, but this does not justify his demeaning it. As the guardian of the neurotic's potential, he must be careful not to exact from him too high a price of self-abnegation; for the neurotic is the person who all his life had to pay dearly for what others got cheaply or for free. As a child he had to buy by sacrificial acts what was his natural due: .parental love. Later on, his brittleness unsuited him for driving hard bargains. As therapists, we ought to protect whatever spirit he has left. We may want him to let go of his neurotic pride, we may even want him to become humble, but not by making him undergo gratuitous humiliations.

Hence the wielding of the therapeutic sledge hammer would be justifiable only if other, gentler, methods were bound to fail. However, this is not the case. A therapy of gentleness which softens up defenses instead of trying to smash them may produce its results slowly, it may demand much patience, but in the end it far outdistances the effects of the purveyors of therapeutic violence.

The forms of therapeutic violence we have discussed so far are massive and obvious; one need not be eagle-eyed to recognize them as such. But psychotherapy is also replete with much more subtle, camouflaged, indirect forms of violence which are much harder to detect. Thus psycho-analysis which claims to be deaf to the solicitations of violence and which disavows authoritarian gestures is not without its taint of surreptitious coercion which may become blatant when a patient challenges its professed innocence. To illustrate this point, we shall present part of a case history which Jean-Paul Sartre published some time ago in his magazine *Temps Modernes*.

The case is that of a twenty-eight-year-old man, designated by his initial "B," who had been in analysis for more than ten years when the following incident occurred. In the middle of a therapy hour, he suddenly pulled out a tape recorder and announced his intention to record the rest of the session "for scientific reasons." The ensuing confrontation, trancribed from the tape, was presented by Sartre verbatim to his readers.

The analyst, introduced under the pseudonym of "Dr. X," panics when the patient produces his taping machine with the following comment: "There is something I want to have clarified. Up to now, I have followed *your* rules, now you *must* try . . ." Without letting B complete his sentence, Dr. X tells him that he is going to "cut off" the hour. B, reversing their roles, interprets the doctor's intent to terminate the session as fear-induced. Dr. X reaches for the phone, with the obvious intention to call for help. B prevents him from using the phone.

It is not clear from the published transcript how threatening the patient's gestures actually were, and to what extent the threat of physical violence about which the doctor keeps talking was conjured up by his own exaggerated fearfulness. At any rate, the utterances of Dr. X sound indeed, as B asserts, as if he was scared to death, whereas B sounds fairly rational. He is angry, but does not seem out of control.

What is actually happening is an attempted *coup d'état*. The patient is quite explicit on this point: "Don't you even want to tell me why you are so angry? It's because all of a sudden I was taking over. Until now, you were used to being in complete control of the situation . . ." The analyst keeps repeating that B is dangerous. B protests; he does not intend any harm. The doctor presses and amplifies his main point: "You are dangerous because you misjudge reality." B refuses to be brow-beaten; he will no longer allow the analyst to define what is real for him. "But what is reality?" he asks ingenuously. "I know one thing—from the point of view of *your* reality—and that's that you are really furious."

In its further course, the confrontation veers, at times, toward low comedy. At one point, after B assures the analyst that he, B, is not the doctor's father, Dr. X, hopefully, attempts a bit of interpretation: "Are you trying to imitate your father at the moment?" B wants none of it: "Of course not—yours! The one I see in your eyes" (referring to X's fearfulness).

The situation, ineptly dealt with by the analyst, escalates to a point where B accuses the doctor of being a charlatan who demands of his charges that they face things but makes them lie supine on a couch where they do not have to confront anything, least of all another person. The indictment continues: "That [putting a person on the couch] is not the way to cure people. It's impossible since, in fact, to live with others is to know how to face them. What did you want me to learn on that couch? The opposite! You had me forget the desire even to try to live with others or to confront anything. And that is what *your* problem is. That is the reason why you want people to stay in that position. It's because you cannot face them . . ."

A bit later, B brings his passionate accusation to its climax: "I couldn't imagine when you were going to give me what I had come to get from you. I was *waiting for your permission*. That's right . . ." Here B has arrived at the heart of the matter. Like Allen Ginsberg and Beatrice, like any neurotic, B was waiting; he was waiting not for a vague, elusive Godot, but for the doctor's specific permission to be well and strong, to live his own reality, and not one prefabricated by others. But in order for this safe-conduct to be effective, it must be genuine, that is, it must be issued by a therapist who has outgrown his infantile needs, who does not want to preserve the umbilical cord joining him to his patient because this cord also feeds *him*, and who need not assert his power by denying the freedom of others.

But let us return to our story. Dr. X, charged by B with trying to get him locked up, admits that he was going to call the police when he reached for the phone. He wanted to have B expelled. B, ironical, still playing analyst, interprets the doctor's intended act as a call for "daddy": "Your daddy is a policeman! And you were phoning your daddy to ask him to come and get me." Dr. X returns to his leitmotiv: springing the tape recorder on him was an act of "physical violence." B seems genuinely surprised. He fails to understand that the doctor gets all wrought up because "someone takes out a little machine which is going to let you understand what is going on here." But he, in his turn, accuses Dr. X of having used violence by coercing him to lie on the coach. Dr. X tries once more to end the interview, but B, who seems to enjoy this settling of accounts, is in no mood to leave. Dr. X keeps repeating, with a hysterical crescendo, that physical violence is in the air, is actually being done to him. B, paternal and mocking by turns, asks the doctor to calm down. There isn't going to be any bloody melodrama. But he blocks the only door, thus effectively preventing Dr. X from leaving without a physical confrontation. The analyst finally screams for help, with a voice that "sounds like a pig being slaughtered." "Help! Murder! Helllp! Helllp!" After a series of screams, the last one of which reaches the paroxysm of a quasi-primal yell, the doctor subsides. A sort of quiet settles, interrupted by bits of more rational talk. They wait for the arrival of the police whom the doctor has asked his wife to summon. Finally, B decides to leave, not without a last sarcastic thrust about "cutting off" the session (castration had been alluded to at earlier stages of their dialogue). Also he makes it clear that *he* is terminating the interview:

"Very well, the session is ended. It's the first one. See you next time. Good-bye, Doctor."

Sartre offers this "psychoanalytic dialogue"—the ironic title having been suggested by B—as a "benign and beneficial scandal." He analyzes, with his usual brilliance, the "farcical reaction of antagonistic reciprocity" where each of the two men psychoanalyzes the other: "It's your father you're imitating; no, it's yours; don't be childish, you're childish," etc.

Unfortunately, we are not offered enough context to understand the incident fully. We are not told what preceded it, we are left ignorant of what followed. We do not know at which stage of B's interminable analysis his revolt (was it a short-lived one?) occurred. We are not told whether he was actually given to outbreaks of violence or to what extent he physically interfered with the doctor's freedom of movement. The incident is not without its funny side. As Sartre notes, it is always amusing to see Grand Guignol punch the Commissioner. What makes the situation particularly incongruous is that the analyst's wild excitement is triggered by such a trivial act: a patient pulls a recording device out of his pocket and declares, with apparent calm, that he wants to tape part of a session.

But whatever the actual context of this odd incident, we cannot dismiss it by simply attaching a psychoanalytic label to it, by calling it an instance of negative transference or a piece of aggressive acting-out, to use the familiar jargon. By using this sort of "explanation," we would not only be playing the analyst's game, buying his version of reality, and thus prejudging, from *his* perspective, what actually happened, we also would explain very little. And by stereotyping the concrete happening, we would de-realize it.

It is precisely against this that B revolts: the prejudgment of the meaning of the therapeutic situation by Dr. X, his implicit, and arrogant, assumption that he knows best what is real, that the real is given and unquestionable, and that a patient who disagrees with him dangerously "misjudges reality." "But what is reality?" B asks, and by his rejoinder makes it clear that the analyst's pontifical talk actually covers up a power struggle. The real question then becomes: whose reality shall prevail? The doctor's or the patient's? Their realities are mutually exclusive because they are at loggerheads, because their relationship lacks the reciprocity which alone would make it genuinely therapeutic. B does not experience the doctor as someone who is affected and moved by his, B's, needs, and hence their relationship becomes one of mutual manipulation, of jockeying for control. Under these conditions, B's lying on the couch is felt by him as an intolerable humiliation, a symbol of his wretched subjection. Whereas more fortunate patients experience the couch as a symbolic womb, the place of their laborious second birth, B perceives only the abdication of his prostrate position, the degradation of a self-surrender which is not based on trust.

Sartre analyzes the confrontation between B and Dr. X as a particular instance of the revolt of the oppressed against their oppressors. He intimates that surreptitious violence is *always* implicit in the psychoanalytic situation in that the quasi-silent and invisible, detached presence of the analyst will transform, in the very mouth of the patient, living words into mere objects. The patient is told that it is his task to discover himself by degrees. The trouble is, B and Sartre tell us, that it is "understood *from the start* that he will discover himself as a passivity, through the intermediary

of this gaze which assesses him and which he cannot grasp."
In this view, the therapist himself becomes a glorified tape
recorder, a recording device which quick-freezes what it
preserves. It is the petrification of the patient's dependency
by the therapist, symbolized by his nailing him to the couch,
which in Sartre's view constitutes the original act of violence.

I think that Sartre's eloquent analysis is mistaken. He
overgeneralizes. His notion of the subtle entrapment of the
patient, of his transformation into a quasi-object, applies
only when therapy has miscarried. A good psychoanalyst,
like any good therapist, far from trying to dominate, will
be guided, largely, by his patient's needs. He will set in
motion a process of mutual modulation in which he, being
stronger, will be more giving and flexible. But he will not
deny the limits of his own tolerance. He will be affected
by his patient's demands, and he will show that he is, but
he will not be twisted out of shape by their urgency.
Frankly, without false guilt, he will refuse those demands
which he does not want to meet. A therapist who behaves
in this way makes the use of violence redundant.

But Sartre is undoubtedly right that violence is often
surreptitiously present in the dealings of analysts with their
patients. What makes the story of B and Dr. X so interest-
ing is that the simple act of introducing a tape recorder
exposes the violence which was implicit in their relationship,
but the existence of which would have been undoubtedly
denied by Dr. X and might have been concealed forever if
B had not pulled his little trick. This sort of camouflaged
therapeutic violence is insidious and hard to deal with.
If the patient obscurely senses its presence and fights back,
he may be accused by the analyst of displaying "negative

transference" or "resistance," or of "acting out." Most analysts are quite adept at casuistry, backed up by a vocabulary of subtle intimidation. They are right, of course, when they note the patient's resistance, but they are often wrong about its motives. An analysand's resistance may stem not only from a neurotic repugnance to deal with the unconscious sources of disturbed behavior; it may also spring from a legitimate reflex of self-defense against the "therapeutic" trespasses of an analyst who is blind to his own abuse of power.

The German poet Novalis has said that every illness is a musical problem which requires a musical resolution. This is most true for those disturbances of the person's harmony which manifest themselves mainly in the psychic realm. Now, undoubtedly a sledge hammer can extract groans and screams from a distempered instrument; but such a hammer is unlikely to restore the instrument to a state where is plays delicate music. Besides, one does not need a hammer to make a heavily defended neurotic emote. I have seen a light knowing touch set off emotional storms which matched in intensity anything described by the advocates of the heavy hand.

In talking about this aspect of psychotherapy, we have to guard against being led astray by metaphors. Our imagery must be chosen with care; it needs to be continuously checked against empirical reality. For instance, once we have defined neurotic defenses as being made of concrete or as armor-plated, it sounds plausible that they can be breached only by some psychic equivalent of dynamite. But it is questionable whether this mineral, inorganic imagery is appropriate for any but the sickest human beings.

With some types of psychotics, we can observe the calcification of a whole life structure, and to describe their shell as ossified may be appropriate. (One such patient dreamed shortly before the outbreak of his psychosis that all animals and plants in his garden had turned to stone.) But should the neurotic, even if his neurosis is severe, be thought of in terms of unyielding, rocklike matter? Certainly not, unless we have convincing proof that gentleness will have as little impact upon his defenses as upon the Rock of Gibraltar. My observations point the other way.

Even among therapists who consider it their major task to set free repressed feelings there is little agreement about the best mode of release. Thus the "primal scream" which is the ultimate good for the Janovian therapist may be looked at as a deplorable short circuit, a "hysterical affect-equivalent," by the orthodox Freudian. And if one watches the activities of Freudian analysts who profess as their goal the de-repression of emotions, it is wondrous to behold in how many ways they manage to circumvent their stated purposes. The same observation applies to therapists from other schools who pursue similar goals.

A case in point is Rogerian counseling. Rogers' notoriety is based on his advocating, in a single-minded way, the recognition and clarification of feelings as the be-all and end-all of therapy. It was Rogers' undoubted merit to have rediscovered the importance of emotion, easily lost sight of in the rarefied atmosphere of academic psychology and its offshoot, the psychological clinic. But having rediscovered the obvious, which, given the intellectualistic myopia of academe, is more meritorious than it sounds, Rogers then went about the business of uncorking feeling in a very mechanical—that is, unfeeling—way. His whole method of "reflecting" feeling is so stereotyped that it is bound to put a severe damper upon the very outpouring of emotion it endeavours to bring about. No wonder that Rogerian counselees are discharged in a hurry. The method keeps aborting the process it sets in motion.

In fact it seems that most therapeutic techniques have built-in dampers, often not recognized as such, which tend to stifle the desired upsurge of buried emotions. Such dampers may be partly desirable, but at least they ought to be seen for what they are. The ultimate damper, of course, is the personality of a therapist who is averse to being exposed to the impact of his patient's raw, crude emotions. Most therapeutic schools provide such therapists with ready-made excuses for cooling the emotional temperature of the therapeutic encounter.

The ways in which the therapist can "cool it" are innumerable. Any interpretation, no matter how correct, any request for factual information to clairify a vague report or memory, any giving of advice or "crisis intervention," no matter how clever, can have the effect of stifling a nascent feeling. Recently a patient of mine told me about a former therapist of his who subtly got across to him that he did not want to be bothered by much raw emoting. For a long time, the patient could not figure out how the message was sent. Finally it occurred to him that the therapist would start every session with the mention of a business item: a bill to be paid, a session to be shifted, a vacation coming up, etc. It dawned upon the patient that this procedure made him feel he was being sprinkled with cold water before even getting started. He began to think of the therapist as the "premature fireman."

Actually, the ritualization of the therapeutic setup itself, the positive aspects of which we mentioned earlier, may have the negative effect of hindering the free flow of emotion, especially in the hands of a rigid therapist. For instance, the usual limitation of the therapeutic session to roughly fifty minutes or the fixed schedule of appointments may contract the expansiveness of patients who feel that they need longer stretches than fifty minutes and more than two or three of even five hours a week for the decompression of their emotions.

We demand of the neurotic that he be ready to undergo great anguish to come to grips with his buried truth. But he can negotiate the infernal journey to self-knowledge only if his willingness to assume anguish is matched by the therapist's readiness to be available when badly needed. A radical therapy—that is, a therapy which goes to the roots of the neurotic's predicament—will expose him to the terror of feeling totally forsaken and alone, but, paradoxically, he can plumb the depths of his aloneness only in the protective presence of a fellow being. The therapist can control, by the sheer quantity of time he allots (assuming this time to be well used), the intensity and depth of a patient's encounter with his reality. The patient, on his part, exerts significant control over this by the amount of time (and money) *he* is ready to commit. Often the limits of the therapist's availability remain untested because of the patient's timidity. Thus a neurotic may fail to ask his therapist for additional time because he fears to impose or is sure to be refused and does not want to deal with the resentment the expected refusal would arouse in him.

A major obstacle to the free flow of feeling is lack of simplicity on the therapist's part. We may look at most psychological theorizing as a making of myths which partly shape and reveal reality, and partly serve to protect us from it; the more complicated the myth, the more protective. Thus psychoanalysis with its baroque conceptual structure may be viewed as an obsessional system with an almost phobic distaste for raw emotion. The phenomena with which psychology deals may be infinitely complex or apt to be perceived as such, their complexity being limited only by the subtlety of the mind that mirrors them, but the basic truths of repressed feelings are simple, often to the point of simple-mindedness. This does not mean that every simplistic notion advanced by a therapist is necessarily true. But it means that the therapist's convolutedness when he addresses his patients is in itself an infallible sign that he has fallen into the trap of intellectualization.

The gentle therapist must be lucid and plain-spoken. He need not be a simpleton.

The gentle therapist aims to create a sort of therapeutic sanctuary where the patient's ghostlike unreality—his denied reality—will manifest itself. This denied reality tends to be elusive. It may surface at first in the most tentative way, as vague forebodings, vaporous misgivings, evanescent dreams, bodily tics, outlandish fantasies, disowned as soon as conceived. Its ghosts are timorous, easily scared away. The neurotic himself is usually too ready to dismiss them. If he concedes them a bit of existence for one moment, he will revoke it the next instant. His ghosts' evanescence, their lack of tangible credentials, makes it easy to send them packing. The neurotic's world is too narrow to offer much of a real stage to these messengers from the imaginary.

On his own, the neurotic lacks nerve to sustain the reality of his ghost. Hence it becomes the job of the therapist to take the side of the neurotic's unreality and to support its claim to be heard. He will embolden the patient to disallow the petty arguments of common sense, which demands objective proof before it recognizes anything as real. He will encourage him not to worry overly about the rules of evidence, but to meet and familiarize himself with the ghost, who will soon turn into a new piece of reality.

How does this realization of the unreal come about? We have already touched upon this process in earlier chapters. We have seen how a person may have a dream or waking vision which seems to him of overwhelming importance while he is experiencing it, but which turns to dust as he comes to. As he returns to his senses—that is, to his former reality—he can no longer conceive how he could have thought that the dream or the vision was anything but trash. He is, in this respect, not unlike a man who has stopped loving a woman and no longer understands what he could possibly have "seen" in her. The trouble is that he has lost the key to the old reality of which his love for this woman was a part. The lights which had endowed her with revelatory magic have gone out or passed on to someone else. Similarly, the awakened dreamer or visionary can no longer find the hidden door to the mysterious realm where his revelation was real. But often the therapist needs only to express his faith in the existence of this hidden realm, or to give some modest pointers, for it to materialize again.

To give a simple example: A patient dreamed that he had set out on a trip to Red China. At the border he ran into some trouble with Chinese guards, mostly because the papers of his female companion were not in order.

This dream seemed very important to the patient while he dreamed it, but upon awakening he found it insignificant. He felt that he must have been mistaken to attach much importance to it. However, he remembered the dream and reported it during his next therapeutic hour. He also mentioned that the dream had seemed very significant at first, during the night, only to lose its luster at daybreak. The therapist made two simple comments. First, he contrasted the patient's adventurous dream voyage to Communist China with the dull, staid routine of his waking life. Then he reminded the patient of another recent dream in which his wife, with whom he believed himself deeply in love, had appeared as an ugly, incredibly fat old hag. He had commented at the time that she must have weighed "at least two tons." The patient let the therapist's words sink in for a while. "Does the China dream try to tell me that I feel dragged down by Carolyn?" he wondered. "Does she interfere with my venturing into new territory because her papers are not in order? Is her shaky sense of identity a millstone around my neck? That must be it." Precisely. A rich vein of half-buried feelings and thoughts had been struck. The patient felt on the brink of living a richer, more adventurous life, but his scared wife, clinging to the status quo, was pulling him back. He recalled that in the dream she had looked like Melvin Laird, the "Secretary of *Defense*." He emphasized "Defense" in an odd, meaningful way. To make sure that the therapist understood him, he added: "Yes, d-e-f-e-n-s-e, that's right! She's always defending things from me." He had the feeling of having traveled, most of his life, with a whole trainload of Melvin Lairds. But it took a dream, and his therapist's support of the dream, to bring this important truth home to him. It is not that he was not acute enough to make, on his own, the simple connections between his dream and his slowly surfacing feelings about the "Lairdishness" of his wife. But he needed the warrant of the therapist to take the dream reality seriously.

Incidentally, on the day preceding his China dream, this patient had taken a step in his waking life which was almost as revolutionary for this slavish follower of etiquette as his dream voyage behind the Great Wall: for the first time in the forty-three years of his life, he had ventured to wear sandals without socks in public! To convey the truly world-shaking significance of this gesture for this patient we may mention that, a few weeks earlier, he had made a short pleasure trip to Miami Beach from which he returned rather crestfallen because nobody had wanted to "swing" with him. When the therapist inquired about some details of his stay, it turned out that the patient had hovered around the periphery of swimming pools and bars attired in a dark business suit. This was his perdurable uniform and it simply had not occurred to him to consider it incongruous for an aspiring Miami swinger.

If the therapist is good at his job of supporting the dream, therapy easily becomes a charmed mystery tour. Propelled by the alchemy of surging emotions, the patient is transported to surreal landscapes where the rules of common reason are suspended. Thus the therapist's room may detach itself from its firm moorings in geometrical space and take off like a floating spaceship—an animated ship which, in harmony with the moods of the transfixed passenger, alters its shape, expands or contracts. The light in the room seems to beat to the same secret tune, alternately darkening or illuminating the objects it plays upon. Pieces of furniture, revealing an unsuspected physiognomy, seem to vibrate with a secret, inner life. And, above all, the face of the therapist begins to pulsate with stroboscopic intensity. One patient said his therapist's face looked like an infinitely mobile rubber mask, in front of which a breeze-blown flame was cavorting, inducing kaleidoscopic changes of expression, "as with a landscape under a quickly moving, intermittent cloud cover." Frequently the therapist's face is transfigured into that of a close relative of the patient. "Your face has become my father's face!" How often have I heard that cry from amazed patients who initially had not seen any resemblance between their fathers' features and mine!

More striking even than its feats of spatial transformation is the magic that therapy practices upon time. To be neurotic means to be the prisoner of a vampirized, empty present and to be haunted by an equally unreal, unlived, and unremembered past. A neurotic, especially of the obsessive type, will cling to the safety of orderly time sequences to keep unruly feelings at bay. He will treat time in the spirit of Newtonian physics as an unilinear, narrow, homogeneous dimension. He will take only tiny cautious steps along the time continuum, putting one foot gingerly in front of the other, never daring really to come to rest. But the impact of therapy dislocates and then dissolves this protective framework of the rationality of clock time. It is exhilarating to watch a neurotic, enslaved by empty duration, freeing himself and performing bolder and bolder leaps in a multidimensional life space no longer subject to the astringent laws of Newtonian physics—a space in which various, and seemingly disparate, moments in time are co-present, supported and bound together by an underlying identity of mood or feeling.

It ought to be mentioned that this abolition of the rationality of time, this presentification of the past, seems to come about quite spontaneously, without the therapist's having to be doctrinaire about the importance of the un-realized past. A case in point is that of a depressed patient who prior to therapy had been a prisoner of abstract time. During the early stages of therapy, he served time by re-porting in detail and chronological order the events of his daily life. When I pointed out this limitation, his temporal frame slowly began to expand until, after about six months, one day he found himself, to his amazement, on a "sort of time train or, better yet, time plane" shuttling back and forth between crucial way stations of a seemingly forgotten past. His eyes closed, he commented on the "total fluidity" of the time-space medium in which he was traveling. The whole experience reminded him vividly of the only LSD trip he had ever taken a few years earlier. He marveled at the fact that he was now able to go tripping "without the artificial wings" supplied by drugs. Then he fell silent, his features working; he was apparently exploring various images. A bit later, he grunted that he was now burrowing, molelike, through a multilevel network of underground tun-nels of snarled complexity. More silence. All of a sudden, he exclaimed: "Wow, things look superclear. It feels as if I could *touch* the past, touch my father," whom, as far back as he could remember, he had never been able to touch. Then he relived, with lifelike vividness, fragments of a scary radio program called "2000 Plus" which he had fol-lowed as a young boy and which dealt with microcosmic worlds existing in the interstices of the atoms of a human body.

"It feels as if I had passed through a time zone," he ex-plained; "the past is *there*. I had cut myself off from it. I see the backyard of my house in New Jersey, and Uncle

Willie. You [pointing to therapist] look as if you had a much younger face like my father at a younger age. Things look much more distinct. Even the Indians on the rug on your wall do not look drab any more. I feel different, as if I saw with the eyes of a child. Things look fresh and fragrant." Another pause. Then he reported having a vision of the stairway of his childhood home going down very deep into the ground. It felt as if the house was a ship, and the stairway was anchoring it to its element. If he wanted to, he could command the earth to go away, to recede, but this would require a very great effort. A further period of silence preceded the next report: "I just went into a dream state. There was something about thirty-one patients. The thirty-first was not saved, was a dog." At this point the patient got scared. He said that if he would do more of what he was then doing, he would start dreaming or go to pieces or become crazy.

A few days later, the same patient relived a totally forgotten dramatic incident of his early childhood which, he felt, changed him "from top to bottom, like in a holographic pattern." On that day his therapy hour started harmlessly enough with his visualizing the room where he had spent his first years. The room seemed to be flooded with a pale blue light which, to him, signified coldness and being alone. He then suddenly shifted his topic and started to talk about an article he had read the night before. According to the author of this article, a noted psychologist, it was futile and senseless to strive to recover in later life the memories of one's early childhood since the schemata by which we apprehend these early experiences do not survive into adulthood. His therapist, refusing to be drawn into this theoretical argument, asked him to return to the pale blue

light enveloping his room. He did. After some more comments about the desolation of his childhood, which he did
not realize so much during the day but was afraid of "seeing"
in the dark of night, he went on to talk about the "blue-ish"
apartment of his grandparents near Central Park. He saw
himself, as a lost four-year-old, wandering down one of its
dark, curved corridors, when all of a sudden, pushing open
a heavy door, he beholds, transfixed, a sight that was to
change his life: his mother in bed with his Uncle Willie,
both of them fully dressed but their faces undone, and he
knowing by their disarray that something is terribly wrong.

At this point the patient interrupted himself: "Funny, I
cannot find any piece of reality to what I am saying." He
was asked what he meant. "I mean it feels so real, but I do
not have any evidence. Perhaps I am making it all up." His
therapist suggested that he stop worrying about evidence,
and simply allow himself to be carried along by the images
he was seeing. He readily acquiesced, saying that he now
saw himself as a scared four-year-old leaving his present,
adult body, warily moving toward the fateful bed in his
grandparents' guest room. But the space on top of the bed
where his mother and uncle would be is now blanked out,
empty, covered by an opaque gauze. The therapist invites
him to look more closely. The patient strains, his face con-
vulsed with fear. "There was dread in this scene," he ex-
claims, "even death. I feel as if a cowl is hovering behind
my back, ready to engulf me. At that moment I split. Part
of me flew out the window in a cuckoo land of fantasy,
part fled down the dark corridor, and the rest of me stays,
a scream stifled in my throat."

The discovery of his mother's betrayal radiated forward
and backward over his whole life, determining his future

and altering his past. "Even the gestures I am now making were conceived at that moment. It is like a freeze-frame in the movies, everything stopped." He knows that his mother will plot to silence him, to make him forget, and that she will bring it off. Then he sees his grandmother's mirror rocking oddly on the wall. The mirror subverts and eclipses the skyline of New York. He feels that his soul has taken refuge in the mirror, and when he gets closer to his soul, the mirror sways. But he does not dare to look at his reflected image because everything is inside him now, even his mother's guilty confusion. He can see it if he looks into the mirror. Dating the onset of his asthma from this day, he sums up: "I am left standing with all these ghosts: the part of me that flew out the window, the part that rushed down the corridor, and the gauzy blank which erased mother and her lover." For him to become whole again, he would have to bring back these ghosts, reabsorb them into his life's fabric, and thus reassemble his shattered self.

In looking back later, this patient observed that the most important contribution of the therapist had been his faith in the reality of the ghosts raised by the half-Faustian, half-Mephistophelean practices of therapy. As a parting gift, the patient gave his doctor a book in which the following passage about the resurrection of the past was underlined: "The being who remembers finds he has become once more a being who once had faith. The immense force, the living energy of these small luminous fires he has rediscovered, rises from the depths of an obscure firmament where their rays reside and lengthen, extending their warmth and grace into the present moment. It is in them alone that he can hope for a reality and a resting place."

The faith of the being who in recovering the past abolishes time is the child's faith in the truth of his immediate experience, his naïve and ardent trust in the truthfulness of his senses. It is this primal faith, predating all specific beliefs, and the confident daring it engenders, which alone emboldens the person to claim his birthright: a reality of his own. To help him vindicate this claim is the most basic, and the most noble, task of psychotherapy.